RiDiCuLoUs

LIVING LIKE
CHRIST
in a
LOVE STARVED
WORLD

with
STUDY GUIDE

by
MIKE BAKER
J.K. JONES
JIM PROBST

TABLE OF CONTENTS

Key to Marginal Icons

▶ College Ministry   🏠 Family Ministry   🆂🅼 Student Ministry

FOREWORD

According to the Oxford English Dictionary, the word ridiculous refers to something that is silly or unreasonable. Labeling something ridiculous is equivalent to judging it absurd, even laughable. It reminds Violet and me of the journey God often calls us on. Ridiculous describes the journey that led us to the Mitumba Slum located in Nairobi Kenya. It wasn't our plan, but it was God's plan. You see my wife Violet and I had been invited to speak at the launch of a neighboring youth program. During the meeting, we met some young people who'd come from the Mitumba slum. The name of this slum immediately caught my attention. In Swahili, Mitumba refers to something that has been rejected, worthless, second hand! God had our attention and soon we were invited to visit the Mitumba slums. These first steps into Mitumba, filled with hesitation, were motivated by the RIDICULOUS love of God!

It's hard to believe it's been 12 years since we first visited the Mitumba slum in 2002. We were completely overwhelmed. Mitumba was truly ridiculous. It was stuffy. It was dirty. There was a horrible stench permeating everything, the result of human waste thrown everywhere. The people were living in the midst of addiction, drugs, alcohol, prostitution and promiscuity. The children were naked, dirty, hungry... neglected. We were broken beyond words by what we experienced. We saw families that needed someone to hold them, talk to them and show them the love of God. The need was overwhelming... but what could we do God? We were one couple. How could we make any difference at all?

But no matter how hard we tried to justify or forget what we saw, God was moving in us to do something. We started small. We taught the children the word of God and gave them food once a week. We realized during the week the children were going back to the streets to beg, steal and sniff glue to numb their hunger pains and hopelessness. We responded by launching an informal school and feeding program. Through it all, we never grew weary of sharing the love of Jesus with children and their families in Mitumba. We were preparing them for a life of service to God outside the slum. Slowly, they began to have God sized dreams that once seemed ridiculous. Next we launched the first church plant in the Mitumba slum. As the church grew, family's lives were changed but we noticed another disturbing trend. Because of the poverty and broken families many children were orphaned. In response, we constructed an orphanage to care of those children abandoned and sleeping in the unforgiving corridors outside. Over time, the church, the school and the children's home grew. God's light was shining in what used to be a very dark place. Romans 4:17 reminds us that God gives life to the dead and calls things that are not as though they were. God was God was transforming lives and calling people back to himself.

Were we accepted in Mitumba in the beginning? Yes and No.

The children loved us but the hardened hearts of the adults did not. They ridiculed us. They laughed at us. They tried to intimidate us. Some even hated us. The light always exposes the darkness and the love we shared was a threat to their sin. They didn't want to change. But because of the ridiculous love of God, we never gave up.

The growth of GOYA ministries during the next several years was amazing. But on November 19, 2011 the government demolished the entire slum with no forewarning. In an instant, we lost everything… everything built by human hands. But what God built remained… his church… his people… his grace. Three months after the destruction, still reeling in chaos, Violet and I visited Eastview Christian Church for the very first time in February of 2012. Pastor Mike preached on generosity and the church giving sacrificially to advance God's kingdom. This sermon was not preached for our benefit, it had been planned a year in advance. But God's timing is always perfect. In response to the teaching, after the regular weekly offering, the congregation took up a 2nd impromptu offering to help us rebuild our ministry. The goal was $40,000. We had no idea what God would do. In one day, Eastview Christian Church donated $225,000 to help us rebuild our ministry. By the end of the week, that amount had grown to $240,000! It was one of the most unreasonable, unexpected moments of my life. In a word… Ridiculous. Over the past 3 years that offering served as a catalyst to rebuild and re-launch GOYA ministries in ways we never could have expected. To learn more, you can visit www.goyaministries.org.

That leads us to you. *This book is about the incredible, uncon - ditional, ridiculous love God has for you and how you will respond.* God called Violet and me to Mitumba and he is calling you to find your MITUMBA. The place right around you, where people are desperate to

FOREWORD

learn about the incredible love of God. What would your community look like if everyone at Eastview embraced their Mitumba? That's our prayer for you and the purpose of this book.

Your Global Partners from Kenya,
Pastor Shadrack & Violet Ogembo

INTRODUCTION

Ridiculous Love. Literally love that is ridiculed — a love that doesn't make sense — a love that can't be explained. This kind of love broke into human existence in the first century through a man named Jesus and the church He established. This love was unlike any before it and unlike anything in the culture it collided with. This new kind of love toppled racial walls, questioned gender inequities, challenged social segregation, and changed the definition of love forever.

Amazingly it was ridiculed instead of received. It was challenged as abnormal. It was threatened instead of embraced. Those espousing this love were killed in order to silence it. Every attempt was made to dispose of the love of Jesus and his church. And yet, the Roman Empire couldn't contain it. Armies couldn't defeat it. World leaders couldn't ignore it. The death of a thousand martyrs couldn't quiet it. And the pagan world couldn't compete with it.

Why? Because as ridiculous as this unconditional love seemed, it was exactly what the world longed for. This love that selflessly sacrificed. This love that served for nothing in return. This love that died for others. This love that had no requirements, conditions, or stipulations. This love that gave without taking. This love that came from God. This love expressed in Jesus' death, burial and resurrection. This love properly lived out in the lives of Christians. This love — this ridiculous love is still what the world longs for.

And by God's design, the church is his instrument of love. Just when the church seems to be marginalized more than ever, just as Christianity seems to be outdated and irrelevant, and just when it seems that this culture will utterly reject the teachings of Christ; the church is actually positioned perfectly to express love. It is actually on display for doing what only it can do. The church was established by love (God so loved the world), in love (Jesus loved us enough to die for us), and for love (It is the love of his followers that defines it). In fact, it is the church, and only the church that can express this love to the world. It may seem like the church will fade as the world continues to reject it. But it won't. For Christ followers can always love — and as ridiculous as it sounds it is this love that the world finds absolutely irresistible.

Mike Baker

Before We Blew It: What is God really like?

1 John 4:19

by Mike Baker

Romantic love is the great ambush of life. Unexpectedly and seemingly overnight, the idea of having an emotional relationship with someone of the opposite sex changes from "yucky" to desirable. A new kind of feeling suddenly wells up in our heart and changes forever our world of relational possibilities. Somewhere around the third or fourth grade, guys notice that girls are pretty, and they don't smell badly like most of their playmates. Simultaneously, girls notice that the boys are loud and sweaty, but kind of cute and entertaining. And love becomes part of the grade school world in a fresh, new way.

At this wonderfully scary stage of life, the warmth of a different kind of love is literally felt in a young heart. It's not the kind of love one has for her family pet, or for pizza, or for her parents, but one that feels ticklish inside and inspires girls to write their beloveds' name and inspires guys to show off. It is absolutely sensational in a most literal way, but here's the rub. There are no guarantees that this love will be reciprocated. As exhilarating as loving another is, it is only half of the relationship equation. Now, we debate in our inner voice: "If I 'love' this girl or that guy, how do I know he or she will love me back?" "What if she don't 'love' me at all." "What if he thinks I'm gross?" In other words, love is risky.

Some give up at this point for fear of rejection.Others charge ahead, needing to have an answer and hoping for best. This is why that initial approach to the one you love is filled with anxiety and apprehension. Will he check "yes" or "no"? Will my friend report back to me that there is mutual interest? Will she accept or reject an invitation to go out on a date? And so the life- long journey of pursuing true love begins and continues until the day we die. Each of us holds a deep desire to love and to be loved. Some shrink from it for fear that they are either unlovely or don't know how to love. Others dive in head first and seem consistently to miss what love is all about. Yet most of us stumble into love and find it be the exhilarating reality our heart's desire indicated it would be.

But where did this all come from? Why this deep soul desire to love and be loved? That is the focus for our reading today. The apostle John proposes the reason for all love in a simple line that we know as I John 4:19. There, he simply says, "We love because he first loved us." All the love you and I have ever experienced or ever will experience begins and ends with the love of God towards us. To be sure, we are called to be loving people as Christ followers. In fact, Jesus indicated this love would be the main way the world would identify us with God, that we "have love one for another" (John 13:35). So we do get to enjoy love for and with one another. But before we even think about loving one another, we have to consider the love of God for us. For His love proceeds and exceeds all others.

In essence, the entire story of mankind is God's continual display of love for us. He sought a love relationship in the garden with our parents, Adam and Eve. He sought a love relationship through covenant with our father Abraham. He sent love letter after love letter through his prophets, calling His people back into loving relationship with Him. But His ultimate display of love came with a gift of inestimable value when God wrote a letter in the person of his son, Jesus. In essence, that letter said then and says now, "Do you love me, yes or no?" The answer really doesn't affect God's response. He has made up His mind. His letter through Jesus Christ says, "I love you no matter what." And it is this love from God to us that is at the root of all the love you and I will ever express or experience. He loves us whether or not we love Him. He loves us even though He doesn't need our love. He loves us to the point of giving His life. He loves us no matter what we do or don't do. He loves us when our love for Him could never equal the love He has given. This is the kind of love most would ridicule and, therefore, a love that can only be described as ridiculous.

Rightly understood, the biblical God does not risk. He knew the outcome way before we reacted to the gift of His Son. But from our human perspective, "For God so loved the world..." is one of the riskiest endeavors ever undertaken. Yet, He loved. He loved fully. He loved without demands. He loved best. He loved first. And it is because we have been loved like this that we can dare to love in a way that others might ridicule.

WEEK ONE
TUESDAY READING

Before We Blew It: What is God really like?
2 Chronicles 33:10-23
by J.K. Jones

King Manasseh mystifies a lot of Bible readers. He was the son of a faithful and courageous revival prompter, King Hezekiah, and the father of one other faithful and courageous revival monarch, King Josiah. Manasseh was absolutely nothing like his father and nothing like his son. Hezekiah and Josiah were covenant-keepers. They were God-lovers who stood against the cultural tide of paganism and corruption. They were kings of obedience and righteousness. Manasseh, on the other hand, was a spiritual mess. His life was marked by persistent disobedience. The Bible puts it succinctly: "He did what was evil in the sight of the LORD" (2 Chronicles 33:2). His reign of fifty-five years (696 to 641 BC) was bathed in idolatry, human sacrifice, the demonic offering of his own sons to pagan gods, and the spilling of innocent blood in the streets of Jerusalem. His story is a difficult one to read.

Some Bible students have compared him with the wicked King Ahaz (2 Kings 16:1-20 and 2 Chronicles 28:1-27). You might recall that Ahaz was the king who manufactured images of the various Baals, like the Mars chocolate people manufacture M&Ms. He was prolific in leading the Israelites away from God. He even closed the doors of the temple and placed pagan altars on every Jerusalem street corner. It is hard to imagine that another king could be more wicked then Ahaz, but if a vote could be taken for the-all-time-most-sinful-monarch, King Manasseh might win by a landslide. Manasseh undid all the reforms that his father, Hezekiah, had accomplished. He intentionally accelerated the dismissal of God as Jehovah and decelerated worship of the King of kings and Lord of lords. He set in place a whole scale persecution of God's prophets. Rabbinic tradition tells us that King Manasseh was the culprit who took the life of the great prophet Isaiah by sawing him in half. How could God possibly show ridiculous love toward this ruler?

We don't know all the details that brought about this mighty tsunami of love. What we do know is that Manasseh was arrested, taken into custody, and deported back to Babylon. A non-biblical document called "the prism of Esar-haddon, King of Assyria" records for us the mention of Manasseh's imprisonment and the required bond in order to be released. Regardless of what the king of Assyria or Manasseh thought, God was the one behind all of this (2 Chronicles 33:11). In that terrible imprisonment, Manasseh, like the prodigal son of Luke 15, came to his senses. The Bible says that Manasseh "entreated the favor of the LORD his God and humbled himself greatly" (33:12). The beauty of the next few words in the biblical narrative cannot be measured. The Chronicles storyteller inserts this magnificent line: "God was moved by his entreaty" (33:13). The extraordinary picture of God, the creator of the universe, bending His loving ear toward Hezekiah and answering his heartfelt petition is nothing short of miraculous. God really listened to Manasseh. This king is the Old Testament's example of "the chief of sinners" (1 Timothy 1:15). Manasseh repents, and God responds. How amazing is that? Talk about ridiculous!

Serious Bible students have observed the omission of the exact penitential prayer of Manasseh. We don't know why this king's most significant prayer is not saved for posterity. Perhaps hearing the dialogue between Saul the persecutor and Jesus, the resurrected Savior, might give us some idea of what Manasseh prayed and how God replied. In Acts 9:1-19, the story of Saul's conversion is told. He is on his way to Damascus in order to arrest any and all who identified with Jesus. Suddenly, Saul encountered a light from heaven. He fell to the ground and heard a voice asking him, "Why are you persecuting me?" Saul replied, "Who are you, Lord?" The answer that came back was astonishing: "I am Jesus, whom you are persecuting." Surely a lot more conversation ensued. Many of us wonder at the prayer of repentance that must have taken place in the heart and words of Saul, but Dr. Luke, the storyteller of Acts, doesn't record it for us. What we do know is that Saul is baptized, given a new name, Paul, and directs the course of his life toward honoring the One that he has previously dishonored. So it is with King Manasseh. His encounter with the Living God caused Manasseh to work at reversing his previous years of apostasy. Maybe your story is just like that. The incredible love of God has a way of recalculating our life's direction.

The simple story of Dawson Trotman, founder of the international discipleship ministry called the Navigators, is a reminder of God's ridiculous love. Daws, in his testimony (*Born to Reproduce*), tells the story of a life spent in pursuing the world's pleasures. He started by stealing dimes from his mother's small bank on top of the dresser and eventually stole hundreds of dollars from his employer. He began to drink heavily at the age of twenty. On four separate occasions, he was so intoxicated that he had to be taken by ambulance to the hospital. On one occasion, a larger than life policeman asked Daws, "Do you like this kind of a life?" Trotman responded, "Sir, I hate it." It was the beginning of a new life for Dawson. God used a small church, two older female Sunday school teachers, and Scripture memory to begin the rebuilding of Dawson's life. God was faithful. His love was sufficient, and Dawson experienced the born again life. God can reclaim any Manasseh. That's how ridiculous His love really is.

WEEK ONE
WEDNESDAY

Before We Blew It: What is God really like?
Zephaniah 3:16-20
by Jim Probst

For decades, pizza has been a powerful elixir to draw students to church activities like moths are drawn to street lights. As a savvy student ministries pastor in the early 90s, I led the charge in a simple outreach event in a friendly neighborhood of Mankato, MN. A trendy movie, a truckload of pizza, and a musty church basement were the main ingredients for an event that would give us ample opportunities to demonstrate the love of Christ to a gangly crowd of church kids and their friends. Clip-art fliers of the event littered the neighborhood, all favors were cashed in, and a few pep talks assured that the movie night would be a hit. In the hour leading up to the event, the "church rats" wandered into the parking lot on cue. Some of the kids from the neighborhood trolled the entrance, looking for confirmation that they were welcome as the flier suggested. And there was Jimmy in the empty lot on the other side of the parking lot.

I had talked with Jimmy several times in the past couple of weeks. He was fourteen going on forty with a lifetime of hardships packed into the past couple of years. While swatting rocks with his aluminum bat, he confessed his interest in church and in Jesus. However, as we got closer to the start of our movie night, he feverishly batted more rocks and kept his distance. The conversation between us would open my eyes to a common perception about God the Father. This would be the first of hundreds of conversations like it over the past twenty years.

Jimmy told me that he would love to join us for the pizza and movie, but he simply could not attend the event. He then poured out stories of brutality and corruption that would make a mobster blush. As he concluded his spontaneous confession, he simply said that he was unfit for church and unloveable. My heart broke. He was so close to church,

SM

15

but so far from comprehending the love of God. He hadn't asked, "What is God really like?" He just acted on his mischaracterization of our Father. If I had the opportunity to talk with him today, I would talk with him about Zephaniah.

Zephaniah was a prophet with a powerful message of contrast between a wicked city and a righteous God. In the three chapters of this Old Testament book, Zephaniah highlights the faithlessness of the masses and the remarkable faithfulness of God. It is fitting that the name Zephaniah means "Yahweh has hidden/protected," suggesting that some would remain faithful and would be protected by their loving Father even in the midst of rampant sin and the turmoil to come. As his message unfolds, God's lovingkindness is displayed to those who call upon His name (Zeph. 3:9) and seek refuge in Him (Zeph. 3:12).

In the third chapter, there are six occurrences of the Hebrew word "qereb." In most translations, this word is translated as "midst." These six occurrences help us to see the remarkable theme of contrast as the ridiculous love of God is displayed (Zeph. 3:3, 3:5, 3:11, 3:12, 3:15, and 3:17). In these passages, we see a just God in the midst of injustice (Zeph. 3:3, 3:5), the LORD protecting the humble in the midst of a haughty people (Zeph. 3:11, 3:12), and a mighty soloist who sings over His own with rejoicing and gladness (Zeph. 3:15,17). Did you catch that?

Zephaniah 3:15-17 reads, "The King of Israel, The Lord, is in your midst; you shall never again fear evil ...The Lord your God is in your midst, a mighty one who will save; he will rejoice over you with gladness; he will quiet you by his love; he will exult over you with loud singing." What an incredible picture of a father with his child. In the Genesis story, God declares on the sixth day of creation that, "it was very good" (Gen. 1:31). How much more incredible that the Father bursts into song, exulting over His children with "loud singing" and "quieting" them "by his love"?

Jimmy didn't know the kind of intimacy, protection, and love expressed in Zephaniah. Jimmy didn't know the ridiculous love of the Father. He was wrapped up in the world's narrative of earning approval and being "good enough" to be loved. That kept him on the outside, looking in. He had not heard this message of God's love. He had only heard of God's disapproval, disappointment, and disregard for those who have made bad choices. That narrative is so consistently and loudly chanted in our society that it is hard to hear the sweet sound of the Father. If we listen carefully, we will hear Him singing. We will be quieted by His love. We will sense Him in our midst, and we will recognize that this Soloist is captivated by His own. He "has taken away the judgments against you, he has cleared away your enemies. The King of Israel, The Lord, is in your midst ..." (Zeph. 3:15).

WEEK ONE
THURSDAY

Before We Blew It: What is God really like?
Song of Songs 7:10
by Charlie Welke

"I am my beloved's,
and his desire is for me."
— Song of Solomon 7.10

In his meditation on the Song of Solomon, Brennan Manning suggests, "A shriveled humanity has a shrunken capacity for receiving the rays of God's love."[1] We are a people hungry for love but gorging ourselves on lesser foods. God's love is the deepest nourishment that we can give our souls, but we often struggle to believe that God even likes us. After blowing it in the Garden, we have forgotten what God is really like.

Today's entertainment industry has taken an interest in old Bible narratives. I am grateful for the recent retelling of the ancient stories in high definition, but I can assure you that the Song of Solomon is not on any "Pastoral Wish List" for an upcoming feature film. The trailer alone for that movie, should it ever come to pass, could not be shown in youth groups, would require accountability meetings afterward, and would probably cause a heart attack at the senior pot luck.

The Song of Solomon is an intimate musing of two lovers over one another. Many Bible scholars suggest that the entire exchange is meant to be an allegory for the intimate relationship between God and His people. Personally, I find it to be a great place to contemplate the love of God *and* the love shared between a husband and wife. Whether an allegory or not, the book speaks to one of the deepest human experiences – intimate love.

An English writer and Catholic theologian, G.K. Chesterton, referred to the desire of God as a 'furious love.' In our day and age, fury invokes images of rage and anger, but its more accurate definition would be the idea of "intense energy" (think about the *fury* of a storm). Song of Solomon 7.10 can give contemplative language to this furious love and desire emanating from God to envelop humanity.

The foundation of the furious longing of God is the Father who is the originating Lover, the Son who is the full self-expression of that Love, and the Spirit who is the original and inexhaustible activity of the Love, drawing the created universe into itself.[2]

After reading Manning's work, I added contemplation of Song of Solomon 7.10 to my morning routine: "*I am my beloved's, and his desire is for me.*" There is a sense in which all of us are looking to be defined by desirability. Part of the human condition is a longing to know that someone out there is interested in me and pleased with me. When we know the furious and unrelenting desire of God, we begin to find our rest and courage in being His beloved. There are at least three truths about God's love from Song of Solomon 7.10 that I find encouraging every day.

First, God's love for me did not start the day that I was born. Human love is constrained by the limitations of the created order – boundaries like time and space. But God's love is an eternal and limitless love; it has always been, and will always be, at its maximum expression (Ephesians 1.4). My belovedness is not new to the cosmic history because God's desire for me has been steady and strong since before even light was spoken into existence.

Secondly, I am encouraged that God's furious desire is unconditional in the present. Human love is seen as a great virtue, and we all strive to practice it as much as possible, but love *is* the nature and character of God (1 John 4.19). He does not have to "dig deep" and find a way to love — it is just who He is. The Lover and King in the Song of Solomon finds every piece of his Bride to be desirable. He scans her up and down, inside and out, and finds her delightful. When I know that the eyes of God are on me in this way, searching me and finding me desirable, I find the daily strength to walk in my belovedness.

The final encouragement comes in realizing that there is an experience of God's desire coming that is far greater than any experiences of Him I have had thus far. My greatest hope in life comes in His promise to me as part of the eternal Bride. As someone who is married and now officiates weddings, I am not sure if there is a more tangible expression of human love then when bride and groom connect in the wedding ceremony. The anticipation of the bride's entrance, the exchanging of vows and rings, the kiss that opens the door to a lifetime of intimacy – weddings are by far our greatest picture of human love. It does not surprise me that God chooses to paint the picture of a wedding in both Genesis and Revelation or that He chooses to talk about us, the Church, as His Bride. The more I think about the Groom's ultimate desire, the more I long to experience it free from the current veils of pain and brokenness.

The furious love of God is an all-consuming and never-ending fire. It was burning before the foundation of the world and before our parents even knew that we were being knit together. It was burning the moment we broke into this world and took our first breaths. It burns every time we roll over, crawl, walk, and run. It has been burning since the first time we blew it and every time we have blown it since. It burned as we began school, got married, and had our first child. And it will burn through the day we retire, the day we hold our first grandchild, and the day our doctor tells us that we are beyond help. On the day we take our last step, utter our final "I love you's" and breathe our last breaths, it will still be burning.

On His day, whenever it shall come to pass, this love that has come to define us will finally satisfy the deepest desires of our soul. The barriers of sin will be removed, and the obstacles to experiencing the fullness of this love will have melted away. We will be ushered into the fiery presence of our doting Groom and finally know what He is really like. Until then, I rest and walk in the truth that,

"I am my beloved's,
and his desire is for me."

---

[1] Manning, Brennan, "The Furious Longing of God," (p. 97). David C. Cook. Colorado Springs, CO: 2009.

[2] Manning (p. 38).

WEEK ONE
FRIDAY READING

Before We Blew It: What is God really like?
John 3:16-17
by Jim Probst

In our reading today, I'd like to draw our attention to the most famous passage in all of Scripture. The English Standard Version (ESV) of John 3:16-17 reads, "For God so loved the world, that he gave his only Son, that whoever believes in him should not perish but have eternal life. For God did not send his Son into the world to condemn the world, but in order that the world might be saved through him." This passage acknowledges our sin, but champions the solution to our "sin problem." Some have committed this passage to memory. Many can share some key phrases, but most misunderstand or misapply this wonderful truth. Filtering this passage through a faulty worldview might sound more like this: "For God was so angry with the world that he sent his Son to enforce the rules, so that we would feel guilty and try harder when things get difficult or when we fail. For God sent his Son into the world to condemn and heap guilt upon it, hoping to overcome indifference and compound sorrow for the things that Jesus suffered, leading them to put forth greater effort to become better people."

I've certainly taken some liberties here. Re-writing this potent passage in this way may help expose the ways we've manipulated its meaning to fit our culture. This culture is sadly lacking Biblical understanding, nearly oblivious to the greatest act of love this world has ever known. Have you noticed that we've distorted the truth of this famous passage in our culture? How often do people outside of the church see Jesus as a good guy who found himself in a difficult circumstance, rather than a Savior destined to address our deepest need? Perhaps there is similar distortion in our churches too!

As we come to the final two days of this initial chapter, it might be helpful to restate how "we blew it" and "what God is really like." An insightful preacher once wrote, "The measure of God's love for us is shown by two things. One is the degree of his sacrifice in saving us from the penalty of our sin. The other is the degree of unworthiness that we had when he saved us" (Piper 28). First, we blew it. Second, God's love precedes our sin, is offered while we are in sin, and overcomes our sin! Simply put, we offered up sin to the Father, and the Father offered up salvation to us through Christ. There is simply no way to overstate our need and His love when we reflect on these two realities.

God's love is anchored in His character, not ours. To say it another way, the Father's love gushes forth from the lover rather than the loved. His love for us was eternally established "before we blew it" by our sin, but not in blissful ignorance of our sin. In fact, "God shows his love for us in that while we were still sinners, Christ died for us" (Romans 5:8). To quote Chip Ingram, "The source of this loving disposition is in God, not in the object. We don't provoke, trick, convince, earn, or win God's love. He doesn't love us because of who we are but because of who he is. His nature and character compel him to express unconditional affection toward us" (181).

What do we do with this teaching today? It is important to understand that the Father's love is demonstrated, not in a void, but in full knowledge of our sin. The reality that "we blew it" did not give the Father an escape clause in His holy contract with us. He continued to pursue us and provide for us in our times of deepest need.

I once heard comedian Ken Davis share a vivid example about this ridiculous love of the Father. He noted that, if a fire were to engulf the crowded theater on any other night, he'd willingly risk his own life to save as many as he could. He would jeopardize his own health to rescue those who could not make their way to the exits. However, he acknowledged that *on this night*, he would not be so heroic for the sake of others. On this particular night, his own children were with him. On this particular night, he would be entirely preoccupied with their safety, not the safety of the crowd. Then Davis paused to drive home the point. God jeopardized the safety of His only begotten Son so that the crowd might be rescued. In fact, there was no question of outcome. The Father knew it would cost the Son his very life in order to save ours. What a humbling thought.

BEFORE WE BLEW IT (What is God really like?)

Our theater is on fire. We've been playing with matches since the very beginning, and we are the guilty party that set the place ablaze. Yet, "God so loved the world, that he gave his only Son, that whoever believes in him should not perish but have eternal life." That's the love of the Father ... a love that "gave his only Son" for you and me. Ridiculous.

WEEK ONE
SATURDAY READING

Before We Blew It: What is God really like?
The Holy Habit of Meditation
by J.K. Jones

We began this week with our senior pastor, Mike Baker, preaching from 1 John 4:19. Perhaps it would be good to remind ourselves at the close of this week what that passage says: "We love because he first loved us." Each Saturday, in this six week study, we want to pause and to give prayerful thought to how some of the Christian disciplines might assist us in experiencing the ridiculous love of God, and, in turn, sharing that same ridiculous love with others. On this first Saturday, let's consider the holy habit of meditation. This spiritual exercise, in particular, has caused a firestorm of controversy. Well-intentioned Christians have dismissed it as grounded in Eastern mysticism or New Age thought. No doubt, some authors and teachers have used the term as an "emptying of the mind." Rather, here we are using the term "meditation" to refer to filling the mind with the Word of God. After all, the Bible elevates the value of meditation. Consider these brief examples: "This Book of the Law shall not depart from your mouth, but you shall *meditate* on it day and night so that you may be careful to do according to all that is written in it" (Joshua 1:8). "...But his delight is in the law of the LORD, and on his law he *meditates* day and night" (Psalm 1:2). "Let the words of my mouth and the *meditation* of my heart be acceptable in your sight, O LORD, my rock and my redeemer" (Psalm 19:14). "...When I remember you upon my bed, and *meditate* on you in the watches of the night..." (Psalm 63:6). "Oh how I love your law! It is my *meditation* all the day" (Psalm 119:97). The primary word in the Old Testament for meditating is "hagah," pronounced "haw-gaw." It emphasizes musing, muttering, or talking to ourselves about God.

The discipline of Christian meditation seeks to bring freshness to our thought life or a renewal of our mind (Romans 12:2). The exercise today specifically targets the holy practice of filling our thought-life with Scripture (think Philippians 4:8). In this case, on this Saturday, we are focusing on 1 John 4:19. To put it into an easily understandable image, we want to eat the Word, chew on it, and allow it to get down into our spiritual bloodstream. Again, so as to be crystal clear, we are filling the mind with Scripture and not emptying it. With that said, let's practice the holy habit of Christian meditation for a few minutes.

1. Reread 1 John 4:19 several times. Notice the verses that surround it. In the literary context in which the verse occurs, John is unfolding five reasons why Christians can love:

   * Because God is love (4:7-8).

   * Because we Christians follow the example of God's love expressed in the sending of Jesus (4:9).

   * Because love is central in witnessing to our faith in Jesus (4:12).

   * Because the sharing of our love with others is one of the assurances that we have actually experienced God's love too (4:13-16).

   * Because God's love for us gives us confidence on the Day of Judgment (4:17-20).

   What part of this little verse grabs you? Remember this discipline is an active one, not a passive one.

2. I'm drawn to the phrase "he first loved..." Pay attention to whatever part of these seven words captures your interest. It could be the simple verb "loved" (past tense – something happened in our past that God did by His own divine initiative), a strong reminder to you of this week's study. God chose to love you and me. Consider how that choice connects with Romans 5:8. Sit on that idea for a minute or two.

3. What does that kind of love look like for you? Ruminate on it. If the love of God had a texture, a taste, a sound, a smell, or an appearance, what would it be like? This is no child's game, though children seem to grasp this practice more readily than adults.

4. Slow down. Take this small verse packed full of incredible theology and turn it into a prayer. What would you want to say to God? In light of "We love because he first loved us," what do you want to pray? Go ahead, pray that prayer.

5. Carry this verse around in your heart throughout the day. Listen for how the Holy Spirit might impress it more deeply into your Jesus-following-life. "We love because he first loved us" ridiculously.

WEEK TWO
MONDAY READING

Behind Closed Doors: Is it possible to love my family
the way God loves me?
1 John 4:7-12
by Mike Baker

If my father were still alive and you could see the two of us
together, your observation would be that we don't look very much alike.
His physical traits and mine were just not similar. Still, I will occasionally catch a glimpse of myself in the mirror (usually when I'm shaving)
or see myself in a photo and be surprised at just how much certain facial
expressions I make look like my dad . Genetically, there are parts of my
dad (however small) that reside in me and cause me to resemble him.
On the other hand, I also strongly resemble my mom's side of the family. When I was little, we attended the same church as my uncle and his
four boys (my cousins), and I was constantly mistaken as one of his
sons. The DNA and physical traits from my mom's side of the family
tree are more dominant in me and determine how I look to this day. But
more than genetics are involved in how a person looks.

People who live together and grow up together as a family over
a lifetime also begin to look like one another in a different way. Even in
cases of adoption and blended families, family members can closely
resemble one another. Their genetic similarities or differences aside,
mannerisms, expressions, and even vocabulary become distinct markers
of the family unit. For example, my youngest son is also a preacher
(though younger and less experienced), and many people remark how
much he looks like me. In fact, upon close examination, he has more of
my wife's genetic attributes, but his mannerisms in preaching make him
look exactly like me. My brother too is a preacher, and many have told
me that they can tell we're related. Again, we don't look alike, but when
he preaches, it's uncanny how much we resemble one another.

So how does all of this family resemblance talk get us to the Scripture we want to consider? Well, our teaching from I John is about a family trait that identifies all believers as members of God's family. Genetically speaking, members of this family vary greatly in their appearances, but spiritually, we are unmistakably identified by the love we share with one another. The question is whether there is hope that we can truly share this spiritual trait with those we share physical traits. In other words, can we really learn to love our family as God has loved us?

Why do I ask? Well, so many of us struggle to love our immediate family members in a ridiculous way. We may find them ridiculous enough, but because we are so familiar with them, know them so well, and share so many intimate memories and experiences, we often find them to be the hardest to love. In extreme cases, some of us have been badly hurt physically or emotionally by our immediate family members, seeming to block any chance at loving them. But according to the apostle John, there is hope. It really is possible (and desired) for us to love our families the way that God has loved us. In fact, the love of God is the family trait that makes this possible.

Take some time to read I John 4:7&8, and let's learn about how we were born to love those in our immediate family because we are related to and called to resemble our Heavenly Father.

Love is born of God. "Love is from God" and "God is love." Love is arguably God's most dominant and recognizable trait (technically, He is equally all of His attributes at once...but don't dwell on that; it'll hurt your brain). You simply couldn't begin to describe Him without mentioning how loving He is. This means that loving one another is when we resemble Him most. In fact, not to love those around us means we don't even know Him, let alone resemble Him as a father. When it comes to those behind the closed doors of my home, God's love trait is evident when I love them.

Love was born to us. Not only does love originate with God, but His love was literally born into the world when Jesus was born. John says, "the love of God was made manifest among us" and "if God so loved us, we also ought to love one another." This is the "why" for loving those in our families. God chose to reveal His love to us in an intimate way through Jesus. This was an astounding act that we often take for granted. He didn't have to. It wasn't easy. We didn't deserve it. We didn't return it. But love was born to us in Christ anyway, and that has made the difference in our lives. Is it possible that, if we loved our family in the way we have been loved (in spite of all the reasons we shouldn't), we could make a difference in their lives?

Love is born in us. At this point, you may be convinced that you need to love your family. But how? Well, commit to cooperate with the spiritual love DNA that is in you. John says that, "whoever loves has been born of God." In fact, we by faith we have been born as sons and daughters of God and, as such, have the genetics within to love as God has loved us. If we are born of God, love will be a trait we exhibit. But we can also choose to watch and to mimic His love, imitate His love as we do our earthly family's mannerisms, expressions, and communications. Pray for strength today to exhibit the love of your spiritual heritage to the people of your earthly heritage. And try to imitate your Dad. In this way, the home becomes the place where we learn to love.

WEEK TWO
TUESDAY READING

Behind Closed Doors: Is it possible to love my family the way God loves me?

2 Samuel 9:1-13

by J.K. Jones

Everyone has a dinner table of some kind. We typically think of it as a routine piece of furniture in our homes marked with functionality, rather than theology. Most of us seldom pause to consider the importance or meaning behind the everyday use of our dinner table. My wife and I were the recipients of a gift from a caring aunt and uncle early in our marriage. They gave us an antique dinner table that had somehow found its way into the Melvin-Sibley High School shop class. It had been mistreated and was in need of some serious restoration. So, my relatives took it upon themselves to reclaim the table. Eventually, it became our table where it provided lasting memories of family meals. That table, though, was lacking any special theological meaning, until one eventful day. I'll tell you about that in a moment. For now, let's simply acknowledge that in both the Old and New Testament, the dinner table takes on a significant, God-centered meaning.

2 Samuel 9:1-13 is our focusing passage today. This brief story inserts the word "table" on four separate occasions (13:7, 10, 11, and 13). King David, out of love for Jonathan, Saul's oldest son and David's dearest friend, wondered if there was anyone left in Saul's household that he could show God's loving kindness. Mike explores that story in this week's video teaching. Specifically, David was looking for the opportunity to be hospitable. Eastern culture enormously valued this expression of love. It is hard for most Westerners to grasp the incredible love behind this one act. The importance of the dinner table in the Bible cannot be overstated. The metaphor of table provides a picture of loving fellowship with others and with God. So, King David, full of love and hospitality, intentionally looked for an opportunity to open his dinner

table to someone in Saul's family. David calls for a servant in the house of Saul by the name of Ziba and asks him this loving question: "Is there not still someone of the house of Saul, that I may show the kindness of God to him?" Ziba responds with these simple words: "There is still a son of Jonathan; he is crippled in his feet" (2 Samuel 9:3). The backstory is found in 2 Samuel 4:4: "Jonathan, the son of Saul, had a son who was crippled in his feet. He was five years old when the news about Saul and Jonathan came from Jezreel (that both were killed by the Philistines), and his nurse took him up and fled, as she fled in her haste, he fell and became lame. And his name was Mephibosheth." So, David invites Mephibosheth to dine at his table as if he were one of his own sons. Some cynics suggest that David only showed this love because he desired to keep an eye on a possible rival to the throne. After all, they suggest, ancient kings typically wiped out all threats to the throne. What makes their view unlikely is the way the story-teller inserts the word "kindness" throughout the narrative (9:1, 3, and 7). It would have been a colossal insult, according to Eastern custom, to invite someone to eat at your table and then to betray them. To dine at the king's table was an honor of the highest kind. It was an expression of great grace, of loving provision, and of merciful protection.

Tie this story of David and Mephibosheth to that of Jesus. The Gospel writers, especially Luke, portray Jesus regularly and often at the dinner table. Think of all those passages that speak of Jesus as dining with Pharisees, tax-collectors, and marginalized people of various kinds (Luke 5:27-32, 7:36-50, 10:38-42, 11:37-54, 14:1-6, 15:1-32, and 19:1-10). Consider the upper room story of Jesus telling the apostles that He must suffer, die, and rise again. At that dinner table, He knows that He will be betrayed and that His disciples will abandon Him. Yet, Jesus shares the Passover feast with them. Fast forward to our day. Every time we share in the Lord's Supper together, we are reminded that our King invites each of us, crippled and broken by sin, to dine with Him. Talk about ridiculous love!

Most all of us recall the terrible day of September 11, 2001. Terrorists attacked, and innocent people died. Many of us can remember where we were and what we were doing. That day is forever etched in our collective memory. Some, in deep hurt and anger, were calling for immediate revenge. Without thought or consideration, all Muslims were grouped together and seen as enemies to the United States and all free-dom-loving people. My wife and I, at the time, were living in Lincoln, Illinois. Our neighbors were Muslims. In fear and concern that they might be targeted, I invited them to stay under our protection. They declined. For several years, we looked for opportunities to show the love of Christ to them. On several occasions, I shoveled their snow and mowed their grass. We had repeatedly invited them to dinner. Eventually, they decided to relocate to the Chicago area in order to be closer to their children and grandchildren. Then, that long awaited day came when they knocked at the door of our house. We were eating a meal with our extended family. Our Muslim friends entered our home carrying gifts. As I recall that day, I'm beginning to cry all over again. They, with emotion, thanked us for loving them and being such good friends. As far as we know, they still have not responded to the Gospel, but we are confident they have heard it and seen it at our dinner table.

 Our homes can be God's instrument to love people the way He does. Will you share your table? Ridiculous love is like that.

WEEK TWO
WEDNESDAY READING

Behind Closed Doors: Is it possible to love my family the way God loves me?
Ephesians 5:22-33
by Jim Probst

The institution of marriage is a lightning rod topic today. From the courthouse to the campus, from politics to parenting, marriage has been debated, defined, and redefined. It has been highly esteemed and hardly acknowledged. For some, it is the foundation of the family, while others see it as a foregone fad. Public opinion appears to be changing, but marriage is originally and ultimately God's idea.

In the book of Genesis, we read, "Then the Lord God said, 'It is not good that the man should be alone; I will make him a helper fit for him' [...] So the Lord God caused a deep sleep to fall upon the man, and while he slept took one of his ribs and closed up its place with flesh. And the rib that the Lord God had taken from the man he made into a woman and brought her to the man [...] Therefore a man shall leave his father and his mother and hold fast to his wife, and they shall become one flesh" (Gen. 2:18-24). Here, in the original paradise, God draws man and woman together for the first wedding.

The final wedding is also recorded in Scripture. As simplistic and serene as the first appears, the last leaves us awe-struck with wonder at the magnitude of this star-studded event. While the first had no guests, no special music, no pomp and circumstance – the last is the ultimate storybook ending with every expectation exceeded. Revelation 19:6-9 gives us a sneak peek at the most dramatic event in the history of the world:

> "Then I heard what seemed to be the voice of a great multitude, like the roar of many waters and like the sound of mighty peals of thunder, crying out,

'Halelujah!
For the Lord reigns.
Let us rejoice and exult and give him the glory,
for the marriage of the Lamb has come,
and his Bride has made herself ready;
it was granted her to clothe herself
With fine linen, bright and pure' –
For the fine linen is the righteous deeds of the saints."

The day is coming when the bride (the church) will be united to the groom (Christ our Lord) in the most glorious occasion of all time.

I suppose some of you are wondering what happened to the pages of your book. Perhaps a page is missing or the editor missed a few things. What could this possibly have to do with "ridiculous" love in the family? There is a point to this historical perspective of weddings. In short, God the Father has woven a wonderful metaphor throughout Scripture and throughout time that paints a picture of the reality that is hard to describe. This metaphor describes a covenant relationship between Christ and His church. It is a picture of love that the world desperately needs to see. And, it is on display in Christ-centered marriages.

Most of us have heard Ephesians 5:21-33 read aloud at a wedding or two. Some of us have studied the passage intently. Many of us read it carefully to tell our other half how to behave, while others may disregard it since it is only addressing married people. I'd like to suggest that this passage is not only prescribing love for us to emulate, but describing Christ's loving relationship with us. Did you catch that? This is more than a "how to" manual for our marriages. It is a "save the date" card with your name on it. There's a wedding celebration coming soon, and we're not only invited, we're the ones walking down the aisle.

At the conclusion of all the great insight about love, respect, submission and "two becoming one flesh" in Ephesians 5:21-31, Paul summarizes, "This mystery is profound, and I am saying that it refers to Christ and the church" (Eph. 5:32). Mystery? Profound? Absolutely. It's also inspiring and challenging to the core. Husbands have the ultimate example in Christ. We are to love our bride like Christ loves His bride (25, 29). There is no higher standard. Wives have plenty to aspire to as well. Their commitment to Christ is to be marked with submission and respect (22, 24, 33) as the church is to act with the Lord.

BEHIND CLOSED DOORS (Can I love family as God loves me?)

      Once again, let's look at the picture that is painted by the faithful marriage of a husband and wife. Those covenant-keeping men and women point beyond *their* marriages to *the* marriage described in Revelation. Our ridiculous love (men) points to Christ. To the degree that we faithfully and sacrificially love our wives, we bear witness to the Groom who was and is and is to come. Our ridiculous love (ladies) provides a tangible expression of the church's response to the loving headship of Christ. This submission and respect is a harbinger of a wedding and marriage beyond our wildest dreams.

WEEK TWO
THURSDAY READING

Behind Closed Doors: Is it possible to love my family the way God loves me?
Ephesians 4:29-5:2
by Jason Smith

How do the people in your neighborhood know that your family is Christian? Do they have to read it on your bumper stickers and t-shirts, or can they see something special about the way your family interacts? Does this concept of Ridiculous Love work in the home? I would contend that one of the reasons that there isn't a large volume of verses particularly focused on family in the New Testament is because the whole of the Christian life is to be lived out in the home.

Jesus told his disciples, "as I have loved you, you also are to love one another. By this all people will know that you are my disciples, if you have love for one another." This virtuous concept of ridiculous love is to be applied and woven into the culture of every Christian household. It is our Family Crest.

As we spend considerable time thinking about the implications of a church turned on to ridiculous love in our community, it reminds me of a quote from D.L. Moody: "A man ought to live so everybody knows he is a Christian…and most of all his family ought to know" (Moody, Dwight L. (2014). *BrainyQuote.com.* Xplore Inc. 2 April 2014.)

This idea of living our lives with ridiculous love cannot merely be a façade for the public portion of our lives. It cannot be like a nice outfit we put on when we want to look good and take off when we want to feel comfortable. It becomes who we are and shows up where we are. A good tree bears good fruit, says Jesus, and a bad tree bears bad fruit (Matthew 7:17-18). Eventually, our deeds find us out, and Jesus warns us repeatedly about acting like something we are not. So in the spirit of his teaching, I warn you that you cannot employ ridiculous love in your life if you have no intention of showing it in your home.

BEHIND CLOSED DOORS (Can I love family as God loves me?)

So, if we are to love our families as Jesus loves us, what does that look like?

In Ephesians 5:1, we are instructed to "be imitators of God, as beloved children." The fact that God has adopted us into his family and loves us so completely and utterly with ridiculous love encourages us to realize that we are to imitate that love in our lives and in our homes. What we are to imitate is indicated in the next verse where Paul continues: "and walk in love as Christ loved us and gave himself up for us." Some English translators put it this way: "and live a life of love, just as Christ loved us and gave himself up for us." It is this calling to sacrifice self and to live in the way of love that creates the environment in which families flourish.

On the contrary, it is usually the elevation of self that is the family's demise. A spouse puts his own happy feelings, as fickle as they are, above his promise to his wife. A child wants his way and turns the home into a battlefield, deploying hateful ultimatums towards worn-down parents in an effort to gain victory over them. Siblings fight, demanding total acquiescence by their brother or sister to their lists of demands and priorities. Spouses trade the "I'll do anything for you" sentiment of their young love for "I've been stuck here all day, now it's your turn to contribute around here while I go have fun!" We each struggle to sacrifice self for the needs and desires of those around us, and oftentimes that struggle is greatest with our own families.

But it is in this context of self-less love that we find this nugget of verses distinctly written about the family in Ephesisans 5:22-6:4 that will be covered in tomorrow's reading. So I want to set the table by noting this essential life rule for all who are a part of a family: love with the ridiculous, self-sacrificing love of Christ, and give up your own privileges, freedoms, and desires for the sake of your family. Husbands, love your wives and give yourself up for her as Christ gave himself up for us (5:25ff.); wives, respect and submit to your husbands (5:22ff.); children, obey your parents (6:1ff.); parents, don't embitter your children (6:4). When everyone gives themselves away, everyone's needs get met. When no one looks out for themselves, each person is better cared for. It's *ridiculous*... but it works.

In Ephesians 4:29-32, Paul gives us a family culture that we can adopt in our homes that helps the individuals in our families become everything God made them to be.

RIDICULOUS

"Do not let any unwholesome talk come out of your mouths, but only what is helpful for building others up according to their needs, that it may benefit those who listen. And do not grieve the Holy Spirit of God, with whom you were sealed for the day of redemption. Get rid of all bitterness, rage and anger, brawling and slander, along with every form of malice. Be kind and compassionate to one another, forgiving each other, just as in Christ God forgave you."

While this is not an exhaustive list of elements central to a Christian culture in the home, it's a great start. If the words we say, the attitudes we hold, and the actions we display reflect the *grace* of these verses, our homes will embrace and embody ridiculous love.

Is it possible to love my family like God loves me? It is essential!

WEEK TWO
FRIDAY READING

Behind Closed Doors: Is it possible to love my family the way God loves me?
Romans 12:4-5
by Jim Probst

About twenty years ago, I had a very formative conversation with a mentor of mine. I asked him how to protect family time as I entered into pastoral ministry. One of his quick comments was to "trade breakfast for dinner" by the way I structured my work schedule. Ministry has a way of expanding beyond boundaries and bleeding into one of the most endangered species of our calendar … family time. For me, "trading breakfast for dinner" means starting work before the kids are awake most days in order to prioritize a priceless dinner/evening with the family most nights. Admittedly, this dining experience ranges from an elaborate home-cooked meal to a five minute feeding frenzy over frozen pizza and a guilt offering of baby carrots. Nonetheless, this time is critical for our family. I trust that most of those who read this book can relate!

On any given evening, you'll likely find us gathered around the table in our familiar seats. We are known for telling stories of the "highs and lows" of the day, laughing, correcting dining etiquette, and looking for those elusive teachable moments. Last night's teachable moment centered on Prom expectations. Tonight's topic could be anything from injuries to missionaries, from hairstyles to French class. My wife and I see the dinner table as a classroom of sorts, and occasionally we get to be the teachers! As we look for teachable moments, we'd do well to have the following message laminated into the dinner table or woven into the fabric of the curtains that adorn the sliding-glass door:

Dear family, I'm asking you to recognize God's grace that has washed over us as we consider how we relate to one another.

Let's work on having an accurate value placed on one another. This starts with looking in the mirror. Don't think too highly of yourself or place yourself above the rest of the family. Instead, have an accurate understanding of your individual value in our family. While no person is above any other member, each mem-ber depends on one another for the health of the whole family. We work better together than we can as individuals. In fact, we were designed to work much like a body with every member functioning in a special way to keep the body working. We each have membership in this family, and this membership is with and for one another.

Love, Dad

Truthfully, this letter is plagiarized. It is nothing more than a reprise of a letter inspired by the Father, written by the Apostle Paul, and carried to the church family in Rome about 2,000 years ago (see Romans 12:3-5). While the entire book covers a wide expression of profound theology, the 12th chapter of Romans has long been one of my favorite sections of Scripture. Here, you find a rich resource of practical teaching on relationships. Think of Romans 12 as a series of concentric circles, starting at the core with you and God (vs. 1-2), expanding to family and church (vs. 3-13), and then ultimately addressing even how to relate to our enemies (vs. 14-21). Over the next three Fridays, we will talk through our opportunities to be "ridiculous" in some of these specific relationships. For now, let's get back to this letter from "Dad."

This potent little passage was intended for the broader church "family," but we would do well to import this teaching within the walls of our homes before exporting our expectations and examples to those beyond our walls. The ESV version of this passage reads,

"For by the grace given to me I say to everyone among you not to think of himself more highly than he ought to think, but to think with sober judgment, each according to the measure of faith that God has assigned. For as in one body we have many members, and the members do not all have the same function, so we, though many, are one body in Christ, and individually members of one another."

BEHIND CLOSED DOORS (Can I love family as God loves me?)

With the passage fresh in our minds, the dinner table theology might look like this:

- **Don't think too highly of yourself.**

  I can't think of any member of the family that is exempt from this word of wisdom. From the parent who wants everything to fit his/her preference to the toddler who is inherently "me" cen- tered, we all need to recognize our tendency to climb upon the throne. Ridiculous love continually defers to the needs of others (Luke 14:8-11) while simultaneously keeping Christ in His rightful place on the throne.

- **Do think of yourself with sober judgment.**

  There is one "root word" in the Greek that is repeated four times in various forms within this verse. The word is expressed in English as "think"(3x) and as "sober judgment" once. We need to think in a manner that is consistent with reality, and that reality revolves around Christ. Any other focal point skews God's design for the (family) body.

- **Each person is unique and uniquely contributes to this "family."**

  We can celebrate our differences in a way that honors our Maker and maximizes each member's contribution.

- **We don't live in isolation but in community as members of one another.**

  In a society that is increasingly individualistic, this "member- ship" is often dismissed or minimized. Yet, God designed us for profound interdependence. Our families can be the training grounds for a "we" mentality in a "me" world.

How's the family doing? Whether it's breakfast or dinner, sports fields or sandboxes, how well are we loving one another? Is it the kind of culture that should be replicated in the generations to come? Is the family life "behind closed doors" the kind of life that should be exported

RIDICULOUS

to a love-starved world? It is by God's grace that some of us can say "yes." It is by God's grace that others can courageously turn the "no" into a "yes." As you navigate the various readings this week, reclaim time with those closest to you. Demonstrate the "ridiculous love" that you've received in Christ and long to deliver to those beyond the borders of your home. Start at home.

WEEK TWO
SATURDAY READING

Behind Closed Doors: Is it possible to love my family the way God loves me?

The Holy Habit of Examination

by J.K. Jones

Self-examination is seldom easy, but is typically beneficial. This all church-study is intended to allow Saturday to be a day of spiritual exercise. I trust you are ready to go to the spiritual gymnasium. Let's start by biblically grounding this particular Christian discipline we are calling self-examination. At the close of Paul's second letter to the Corinthians, he writes these challenging words: "Examine yourselves, to see whether you are in the faith. Test yourselves. Or do you not realize this about yourselves, that Jesus Christ is in you? – unless indeed you fail to meet the test! I hope you will find out that we have not failed the test" (2 Corinthians 13:5-6). At the heart of this section of Scripture is Paul's deep and abiding desire that the Corinthians, his spiritual children, live godly lives. He invites and encourages them to take a good look into their relationship with Jesus Christ. Fundamentally, in the larger context of the letter (chapters 10-13), Paul addresses their criticism of him as not being a genuine apostle. His argument goes something like this: "If I'm not a genuine apostle, then you are not genuine followers of Jesus. After all, I'm the one who led you to saving faith in Christ." If Paul was a counterfeit, then so were they. Therefore, Paul invites these less-than-perfect-Jesus-followers to do some spiritual examination. Consider Psalm 32 and 51 as examples of David's willingness to invite God into the examination process.

Self-examination is at the very center of a healthy relationship with Jesus. This exercise is not some morbid introspection: "Does God love me? Does He not love me? Am I saved? Am I not saved?" Rather, this specific discipline is the mark of someone who desires to cooperate with God's intention to grow to look more and more like Jesus. A lot of

RIDICULOUS

 Jesus-followers find this very exercise a good practice at the close of the day. It assists us in exploring whether we have loved God and our neighbor as ourselves. For example, each evening we could ask ourselves, "Have I been responsive to the presence of God today? Have my thoughts, words, and actions been pleasing to the God I love? Have I hurt anyone today? Am I in need of seeking God's forgiveness and their forgiveness?"

For years, I have a kept a list of twenty questions (or more) in the front of my Bible that help me in the process of regular self-examination. I offer these prompting questions today in order to help each of us lovingly and graciously stretch and build our spiritual muscles. I think of this as my self-audit. Each question gives the Holy Spirit the chance to speak into my life and to point out anything that needs correction, confession, or repentance. It also affords me the opportunity to celebrate, to be encouraged, and to be reminded of some specific area in my life that God, by His grace, is growing.

1. Am I closer to Jesus now then at my conversion?

2. Have I consistently trained today to be more grace-centered and less legalistic?

3. Did my family see God in me today?

4. Can I be trusted? Have I been trustworthy today?

5. Have I been a slave to dress, friends, work, or habits today?

6. Did I exaggerate, or was I honest today in my words and actions?

7. Did I spend time in Scripture today? Did Scripture live in me today?

8. Did my passion, personality, and giftedness work together today to bring God praise?

9. Did I grow toward "praying without ceasing"? Did I stay in-touch with God today?

BEHIND CLOSED DOORS (Can I love family as God loves me?)

10. Was I self-pitying, self-justifying, or self-conscious today?

11. Did I grow in awe and wonder of God today?

12. Was I a trusted steward of what God has entrusted to me today?

13. Did I get up on time and to bed on time in order to be alert to God?

14. Did I maintain a balanced diet physically, emotionally, intellectually, and spiritually today?

15. How did I manage my free time today? Was my time under His Lordship?

16. Did I speak openly today about my relationship with Jesus? Did I miss an opportunity? Who did I serve in the name of Jesus today?

17. Have I been jealous, impure, or irritable toward anyone today?

18. Have I developed an unholy habit today of grumbling or complaining? Did I celebrate anything?

19. Have I been obedient in the little things today (i.e. kept my promises)?

20. Have I been anywhere, seen anything, done anything, or heard anything that was not God-honoring today? Did I grieve over sin today? Did I rejoice over righteousness today?

Perhaps it would be wise to put these questions in your Bible or in some strategic location where you can be reminded of the practice of self-examination. After all, what we are pursuing in this all-church study is growing in the practice of sharing God's ridiculous love in a way that makes Him irresistible. A little test now and then can help us love like that.

WEEK THREE
MONDAY READING

Between the Pews: How do I love an imperfect church?
1 John 4:20-21
by Mike Baker

Third pew on the left, middle of the row. That's where Lillian, the elderly matron of this small country church has been sitting every Sunday for over forty years. Christmas. Easter. Summertime. Cold of winter. Rains of Spring. You'll find her there. On occasion, an unknowing visitor comes dangerously close to nudging her to another location, but, through it all, this has been her place. She likes the view from here.

From here, she can see the preacher clearly as he brings the Sunday message. She's seen preachers come and go, and, frankly, she's heard better than the one she is currently listening to, but she smiles and nods appropriately as he speaks. Besides, her view is not only of the small stage behind the communion table. From here, she can see those imperfect people she attends church with — people who represent the relationships that take place between the pews.

Looking to her left, she sees the pianist who has just finished playing the communion hymn. She seems nice enough with her Sunday dress and pearls, but as a local real estate agent, she is known as a tenacious and aggressive business woman who doesn't always exhibit the fruit of the Spirit. She may be all smiles on Sunday, but during the week, she's as cut-throat as it gets.

The noise coming from the right of the auditorium is a young mother wrestling with two toddlers. There is no dad to help because, well, she's never been married, and rumor has it that each child has a different father. She is a member of the church and a really nice girl, but her past literally crawls all over her every Sunday.

Glancing over her shoulder, our church matron catches a glimpse of her "church rival," if there can be such a thing. A few years back, they had some falling out over who should be in charge of an all-church dinner or some such thing, and their relationship has been reduced to a forced smile and cordial "good morning" ever since.

Finally, she cannot miss the young man who sits directly in front of her each Sunday. His long beard and t-shirt-jean attire are second only to his numerous tattoos in being a distraction. This and the frequent (and very loud) "Amens" that he offers up all during the service reminds her that he is just different than the rest.

John 4:20-21 says that we are to love these imperfect people between the pews: "This is the commandment we have from him: whoever loves God must also love his brother." But how can we love a church full of imperfect people? How can we love those who seem to be hypocrites? How can we love those who have past sins that follow them wherever they go? How can we love those we disagree with? And how can we love those who are nothing like us?

We love imperfect people by constantly reminding ourselves how God has loved us in Christ. How can God love me when, in hypocrisy, I sing, "I surrender all"? How can God love me even in my worst and most sinful moments from my past (yes, He knows)? How can God love me when my ways are not His ways, and in my human weakness I'm nothing like him? I'm not sure we can answer how He could love us. But He does. So we can try to offer to others what we have received so freely.

When we take this attitude, life seems to take care of the rest. As we live together in the family of God, circumstances have a way of bringing out a ridiculous love for those we sing with, share with, grow with, and labor with. In fact, it is precisely the unpredictability of life together that provides our best opportunities to love one another.

Until a year ago, Lillian sat next to her husband every Sunday. That's when an unexpected heart attack took him home to be with the Lord. And that's when she learned about love. The pianist cancelled a business trip to play at his funeral. The noisy kids made construction paper and crayon sympathy cards. The woman she was at odds with brought a pie by the house and stayed for tea. And the tattooed young man gave Lillian a hug and cried with her. He has mowed her lawn every week since the funeral. Lillian loves these people!

And there it is.: the ridiculous love of Christ displayed in the greatly loved and imperfect people of God right there between the pews, third pew on the left, middle of the row.

WEEK 3
TUESDAY READING

Between the Pews: How do I love an imperfect church?
Numbers 12:1-16
by J.K. Jones

Believe it or not, accept it or not, God's perfect love empowers us to love imperfect people, especially His church. This week's video teaching focused on Numbers 12:1-16 and the relationship between siblings: specifically Moses, Aaron, and Miriam. It is right to think of those three and the millions who are traveling with them through the wilderness as the people of God or a congregation. Mike's observation is an accurate one: "It is really easy to have conflict between people, even if they are brothers and sisters in real life." If Numbers 12:1-16 has gotten a little stale for you, go back right now and re-read it. Perhaps it would be wise to read it from a translation that you typically don't use.

Scripture's willingness to talk openly and honestly about conflict is one of the major reasons why I'm drawn to it as a reader. God, as the divine author, with multiple contributors, never glosses over the muck and mess. Briefly consider all the episodes that are marred with conflict. From the beginning, in Genesis 3, once Satan persuades Eve to eat the forbidden fruit, the blame game begins. Adam blames Eve; Eve blames the enemy, and God must initiate the long and faithful reconstruction of what has now been fractured by sin. Soon after, Cain kills Abel (Genesis 4). God soon regrets that He had ever made man, and His heart is grieved (Genesis 6:6). The global flood described in Genesis 6 is a vivid reminder of the conflict of sin that had swept through the entire human race. Not all conflict is sin, but this particular scene in the unfolding story of God's plan to send a Savior is a powerful reminder of imperfect people in need of a perfect love. No sooner does the rain stop, the ark find a resting place, the rainbow become God's power point of promise, and the family of Noah exit the boat in order to begin a new life, then, once again, conflict entered when Noah drank too much, and Ham saw too much.

Again, Scripture is packed full of stories that resemble the angst and envy of Miriam and Aaron toward Moses. No one can read through the historical books of Joshua, Judges, Ruth, 1 and 2 Samuel, 1 and 2 Kings, 1 and 2 Chronicles, Ezra, Nehemiah, and Esther and not encounter conflict after conflict after conflict. Even a simple reading of the four Gospels, Acts, and the letters written to local congregations and settings by Paul, Peter, James, John, and Jude immediately reveals the friction and fracture that existed among Jesus' own disciples and those who would become a part of His church. Before we return to Numbers 12, just remind yourself of the cataclysmic war that John describes in Revelation. These words alone are ample evidence that there is no shortage of imperfect people in need of a perfect love:

> "And to the angel of the church in Thyatira write: 'The words of the Son of God, who has eyes like a flame of fire, and whose feet are like burnished bronze. I know your works...But I have this against you, that you tolerate that woman Jezebel, who calls herself a prophetess and is teaching and seducing my servants to practice sexual immorality and to eat food sacrificed to idols'" (Revelation 2:18-20).

All of these passages and more are stark reminders of the subtleties and strategies of the enemy to divide and conquer God's people. Only God's love can hold us together. So, here we are on this Tuesday, back full-circle to Moses, Aaron, and Miriam. I have often wondered if their upbringing was marred with envy. Aaron and Miriam are raised in a Hebrew home, foreigners in the land, surrounded by oppression and slavery, barely able to make ends meet. I would guess that bedtime often saw their stomachs aching for more food. I know a little about going to bed hungry and something about envying those families that had abundant food in that small town where I grew up. Moses, on the other hand, was raised in Pharaoh's palace, with all the rights and privileges that wealth and power could bring. The Bible doesn't speak to this, but it does speak to the leadership envy that lived in the heart of Aaron and Miriam. Fortunately for them, Moses had spent forty years in the Midian wilderness getting to know the nature and character of God. Moses's heart is shaped in that desert to resemble the very heart of God. His compassion and love for his people becomes evident in the Exodus story. Time and time again, Moses pleads to God, on behalf of Israel, not to destroy His people. That loving heart is the very one that makes the difference in the insurrection of Aaron and Miriam toward Moses. I implore you not to miss this. In Moses' words to God, on behalf of Miriam, is the secret of a loving heart: "O God, please heal her – please" (Numbers 12:13). She doesn't deserve it. She can't earn it. Moses freely gives it. Why? The answer is clear. God had transplanted His heart into Moses. That same God is able to do the needed surgery on you and me. To love an imperfect people with a perfect love, even in the church, is possible because we have a God who loves ridiculously.

WEEK THREE
WEDNESDAY READING

Between the Pews: How do I love an imperfect church?
1 John 3:16-18
by Jim Probst

WARNING: The following message may be found deeply con-victing. Read at your own risk. Side effects include soul search-ing, prayerful contemplation, redness of the eyes and actions consistent with statements. As these symptoms persist, please recognize you are under the tender care of the Great Physician.

One of the greatest obstacles to following Christ is the example of Christians. Have you ever stopped to think about that? As I interact with those who are indifferent or even hostile to Christianity, I often find that they respect or even appreciate the teachings of Christ. What they cannot get past is a searing image of Christians who have let them down, confirmed their skepticism, or shown some level of hypocrisy that puts the messenger at odds with the message. Do you have the same kind of honest feedback from those who are not Christians? Let's take it a bit fur-ther. Do *Christians* lose heart because of Christ or because of people who bear the name of Christ? Most of the counseling in my office revolves around the wounds one Christian inflicts on another. My hunch is that many of the wounds you and I bear are from "friendly fire" as well.

Rather than running from the hard truth, John writes to the church, specifically addressing these difficult realities in the third chap-ter of 1 John. Here, he draws a sharp distinction between those who fol-low after Christ and those who don't. In verse 10, we read, "By this it is evident who are the children of God, and who are the children of the devil: whoever does not practice righteousness is not of God, nor is the one who does not love his brother." For the sake of this teaching today, we'll set aside the concept of "practicing righteousness" for another day, and we will focus on the second part of this admonition – loving our brothers. John further develops the theme of loving one another a few verses later: "By this we know love, that he laid down his life for us, and we ought to lay down our lives for the brothers. But if anyone has the world's goods and sees his brother in need, yet closes his heart against him, how does God's love abide in him? Little children, let us not love in word or talk but in deed and in truth" (1 John 3:16-18).

Every great leader takes people on a journey rather than telling them where to go. In other words, leaders concern themselves with moral authority more than positional authority. The Apostle Paul's charge to "Be imitators of me, as I am of Christ" comes to mind (1 Cor. 11:1). When we think of the great expectations that Christ has for us, we can be confident that they were preceded by great examples. Here in 1 John 3:16, we are reminded that the standard of loving others is set by Jesus as He "laid down his life for us." His example is the basis for our imitation. We are not simply encouraged to appreciate His sacrifice for us, but to emulate it. Thankfully, the passage continues with some "baby steps" to give us some holy momentum.

In verse 17, we are encouraged to meet the needs of a "brother" rather than to "close our heart against him." If I'm willing to slow my mind down and to replay a typical week, I'll find areas where I've "closed my heart" to the needs of those around me. Sometimes I miss the God-ordained ministry opportunities before me because I'm busy with my own pre-conceived ideas about what needs to be done. Other times, there is an even uglier excuse. Occasionally, I'm simply selfish. I'm guessing I'm not alone on this one. This little verse could keep me awake most nights and could keep me busy the rest of my life. I don't want to dismiss it too quickly. The verse concludes with a painful rhetorical question: "How does God's love abide in him?"

Even as I write this daily reading, I'm tempted to rescue the tension. I want to jump to grace and let you and me off the hook, but that's not what comes next. The next verse continues to hit us right between the eyes. Maybe we should look at the "warning" notice at the beginning of this section!

Verse 18 reads, "...let us not love in word or talk but in deed and in truth." Let's be honest; talk is easier. We can speak encouraging words to people without depleting our bank accounts, calendars, or other precious commodities. But John is reminding us that "talk is cheap."

Our works give weight to our words. From time to time, I have the privilege of seeing these weighty works in action.

On many occasions, I've been the stealth accomplice to a great work. I love the moments when someone gives me an envelope of cash with instructions to deliver it to a member in need. Those moments of delivery are precious as the recipient visibly lightens up at the thought of eased financial burdens. He also lights up at the thought of an anonymous friend who loves him enough to see and meet his needs. This is the church simply being the church.

How do we love an imperfect church? Bit by bit. Day by day. Need by need. And as our works support our words, we'll find that the members and skeptics alike will find us to be ridiculous. And that's a good thing!

WEEK THREE
THURSDAY READING

Between the Pews: How do I love an imperfect church?
John 13:34-35
by Caleb Baker

Jesus gives this simply put, yet incredibly challenging commandment to His followers and believers, He says, "Just as I have loved you, you also are to love one another." He even goes further to say that it's our love for one another that will set us apart from the world. In a sense, Jesus is saying that our love for our brothers and sisters is to be our nametag; it's to be our entire résumé. It becomes so easy for us to get distracted from that, doesn't it? The disagreements or misunderstandings can have such a foothold on our churches. We get sidetracked from our identity and our unrestrained focus on Christ by the always seemingly important symptoms of our brokenness. However, this brokenness isn't what we are to latch onto; it isn't what our concentration should be centered on. As a fearless church family, our focus needs to be on this ridiculous love that God has lavished upon us and the ridiculous love that we are express toward one another. Jesus tells us in John 13 that *this* love, this ridiculous love for one another, is how people will know the type of people we are; it's what we're to be associated with.

I love the intentionality of Jesus' teaching and His use of the word "new" in John 13; Jesus says that this is a "new" or fresh commandment. In other words, the way we love our brothers and sisters in Christ was designed to be a fresh way of life in this world. It doesn't take but two minutes to look on a news channel or to read online articles or to look in workplaces or schools or homes and see that this commandment Jesus gives us in John 13 isn't fitting in with the norm, so to speak. Jesus knows that. That's why He said this is a new commandment. Jesus is telling us that it's going to be different than everyone else. He is telling us that the type of love we have for one another within our church family shouldn't look like the rest of the world; it should raise

SM

55

some eyebrows, it should spark conversations of intrigue, it should seem ridiculous.

I had a close friend of mine in high school start coming to church with me when we were around sixteen years old or so. He came from a very rough home life: dad in prison, mom working multiple jobs to make things work, brothers and sisters in and out of the house and in and out of jail. He didn't have much of a faith backbone at all; he had never been involved in a church and didn't have much of an idea of Jesus or who He was. The first couple of weeks he came to church with me, he was widely accepted. The high schoolers in my youth group brought him in and loved him so unbelievably well. After coming to church with me for about three months, he decided to get baptized, and my youth pastor baptized him and took him under his wing like they were family. We would leave church every week, and he would look at me and say, "Do you tell these people they have to be nice to me? Do you tell them how to encourage me or the things that I like? Why do they love me so much?" The way that my youth group loved him truly seemed ridiculous to him; he couldn't explain it away, and he couldn't make sense of it. He was convinced that I was paying them off to be nice to him, but as it kept happening and they kept loving him and accepting him, his hard heart melted, and he was experiencing Jesus working in his life through all of these brothers and sisters. They took Jesus's new commandment seriously; they believed that my friend was only ever going to know Jesus if he saw Jesus in them. They had no reason to accept him. He didn't look like them, he didn't grow up in nice neighborhoods like them, he didn't have a mom and dad and eight cars like them, but he needed Jesus *just* like them, and they gave him a picture of that. They really did love him ridiculously.

This new commandment from John 13 is of the utmost importance. I love that this commandment to love one another well is sandwiched in John 13 between Jesus telling his disciples that He will be betrayed by one of them and telling Peter that He's going to be denied by him. The structure of John 13 preaches to me a lot; Jesus is saying that this new commandment, this commandment to love each other like He has loved us, is the only thing that's going to be able to carry us through the hard things that we go through. Jesus's foretelling of the betrayal and the denial is two of the lowest points for His disciples. The only thing that is strong enough to hold all of this together is to point our eyes toward Christ and to love each other ridiculously, through the good times and the bad. Oh, he also covers how our focus on Christ will keep us from getting bogged down by a difference of preference or opinion or crushed by the constant flow of gossip and comparison. We can come together and live by this new, fresh commandment that Jesus gives us to love one another in this world that desperately needs us to.

WEEK THREE
FRIDAY READING

Between the Pews: How do I love an imperfect church?
Romans 12:9-13
by Jim Probst

Eastview Christian Church is striving to become "A fearless church of Christ followers whose ridiculous love and dangerous witness is irresistible." Of these fourteen visionary words, the three we hear most often in our community of faith are "fearless," "ridiculous," and "dangerous." But in this daily reading, I'd like to explain how "ridiculous" leads to "irresistibility." While we are certainly an imperfect church, our love for one another can be remarkably attractive.

For nearly twenty years, I've been preoccupied with getting a clearer picture of God's design for community. Throughout my faith journey, I've firmly believed that authentic Christianity is absolutely compelling and that the world simply cannot compete with what the true Church has to offer. One of my passions is to catch glimpses of genuine, authentic faith on display in community. With this in mind, it's humbling to admit that Romans 12 snuck up on me this past year. I had been looking for a fresh perspective on "authentic Biblical community". I was searching for Biblical instruction that would paint a picture of authentic community ... the kind of fellowship that sets the church apart from the myriads of phonies in our culture. Then I read the familiar words of Romans 12 with fresh eyes:

> "Let love be genuine. Abhor what is evil; hold fast to what is good. Love one another with brotherly affection. Outdo one another in showing honor. Do not be slothful in zeal, be fervent in spirit, serve the Lord. Rejoice in hope, be patient in tribulation, be constant in prayer. Contribute to the needs of the saints and seek to show hospitality." (Romans 12:9-13, ESV).

It appears that Paul was preoccupied with authentic community too. Influenced by the Holy Spirit, he laid out some specific instructions to the church in Rome about "Biblical community."

BETWEEN THE PEWS (How do I love an imperfect church?)

It is important to recognize that the entire chapter is about authentic Christianity, lived out in various contexts and segments of community. But in this little section of chapter 12 (verses 9-13), we see a crystal clear call to the kind of community that is attractive ... maybe even irresistible. According to this passage, Paul notes "12 ELEMENTS OF AUTHENTIC BIBLICAL COMMUNITY":

1. **Love genuinely** (vs. 9). This requires sincerity, void of hypocrisy.

2. **Abhor evil** (vs. 9). It is interesting that the instruction to "love" is immediately followed by the words, "Abhor what is evil." Yet, this is a critical component of our community.

3. **Cling to goodness** (vs. 9). Good is incompatible with evil. What do we recoil from, and to what will we hold fast?

4. **Be devoted to one another with brotherly affection** (vs. 10). There is a tender affection that unites "brothers and sisters" in Christ.

5. **Outdo one another with honor** (vs. 10). This is the second "one another" of this verse, noting that affection and honor are closely aligned.

6. **Don't lack zeal** (vs. 11). Christian service is not a passive endeavor.

7. **Serve fervently** (vs. 11). This is an intense activity, not looking for casual consumerism, but passionate participation.

8. **Rejoice in hope** (vs. 12). This is a confident expression of Christ's return.

9. **Be patient in tribulation** (vs. 12). Our hope remains in trying times. Patience is not passive tolerance, but active endurance.

10. **Pray constantly** (vs. 12). Prayer helps us to persevere, reminding us of our source of hope.

11. **Contribute generously** (vs. 13). Generosity is one of the great hallmarks of faith.

12. Show hospitality (vs. 13). As generosity is shown within the community of faith, hospitality is extended to the greater community, by faith.

Pause with me for a moment and dream about a fellowship marked by the actions listed above. In the midst of messy and imperfect lives, how incredible is the witness of a community that unconditionally loves, outdoes one another in honor, serves with all their might, rejoices in hope, and displays patience in all circumstances? Imagine a place where people cling to all that is good; they break from the casual Christianity of the day with uncommon zeal; they pray as if it really mattered, and they overwhelm people with generosity! We couldn't keep people away from such a place!

Now, back to our current condition. These words sound great, and we would love to enter into such a place. But just look at the people we're working with at our church! Think about the wrecked lives in my small group alone. Alright, in my family alone! Our default response is to say, "yeah, but ..." to the very responsibilities listed above. We are often quick to recognize the problem and slow to be part of the solution. And, we're not alone. Have you considered that most of the New Testament is written to broken people in messy churches? Heather Zempel wisely notes, "Messy community is not the exception to the rule; it's the rule. The good news is that mess, when engaged rightly, can be the very thing that brings what we most want ... community and growth" (*Community is Messy* 28). I think she's right. I don't think God is surprised by the difficulties of community. I think it is the crucible He uses for shaping and refining us.

God, in His wisdom, designed us to be in community. His call for us to be authentic is not at odds with the reality of our imperfection. He pulls together all of our dysfunction, warts, and shortfalls, and He calls us His bride (see Eph. 5:22-33). It is an imperfect Church, filled with imperfect people, guided by imperfect leaders with imperfect policies and programs. Yet, the Groom finds His bride irresistible. Let's take a closer look at her ourselves ... we might just see what He sees.

WEEK THREE
SATURDAY READING

Between the Pews: How do I love an imperfect church?
The Holy Habit of Prayer
by J.K. Jones

Prayer is the Jesus-follower's essential ingredient. What blood is to the body, and what oxygen is to the lungs, prayer is to the interior world. We cannot survive very long without it. There is something called the rule of three. It goes like this. Most of us can last three weeks without food, 3 days without water, and 3 minutes with oxygen. However, it is my conviction that Jesus-followers cannot last three seconds without prayer. No doubt we try. So often, our routine lives are consumed with *our* calendars, *our* agendas, and *our* strength. These Saturday readings are intended to encourage us to practice a particular Christian discipline in light of the theme of the week. This week, we have been studying how God's love empowers us to love an imperfect church. Prayer is the just-right spiritual exercise. There are, within the pages of the New Testament, at least four different words for prayer. Without getting too far afield of today's focus, those words include the following:

1. *Proseuche* – General prayer. It is the noun that is most used in the New Testament to describe prayer. We would find it in places like Matthew 21:22, Luke 6:12, Ephesians 6:18, Philippians 4:6, 1 Timothy 2:1, 5:5, and James 5:17. The verb form is found all over the Gospels and Acts.
2. *Enteuxis* – This is the word that describes the relationship of a praying person to our Creator-Redeemer God. It paints a picture of the lesser petitioning the greater for something. See 1 Timothy 4:5.
3. *Deesis* – This noun is closely related to the previous one (#2). It particularly emphasizes the "asking" piece of prayer. Sometimes it is translated as "supplication" or "request."

4. *Euche* – This one is tough to define. Perhaps the best way to make it clear is to offer an example: "The *prayer* of a righteous person has great power as it is working" (James 5:16). In the context, James is describing the prayer life of Elijah based on 1 Kings 18:41-46. In the larger story, a vow had been made by God to King Ahab through Elijah that no rain would fall, except "by the word of the LORD" (1 Kings 17:1). The idea that gives shape to this word is the picture of a vow. That's exactly how it is translated in Acts 18:18: "After this, Paul stayed many days longer and then took leave of the brothers and set sail for Syria, and with him Priscilla and Aquila. At Cenchreae he had cut his hair, for he was under a *vow*." Paul had offered a specific vow-like prayer.

Let's not make this more complicated than necessary. Prayer is simply creating a holy conversation with God. It includes both talking and listening. The Bible is saturated with examples of prayer practice. There are 650 specific prayers in the Bible, and at least 50 of those are significant in content and size. It is hard to narrow down a list, but perhaps these can help: Genesis 4:26, Deuteronomy 9:25-29, 1 Kings 3:4-15, Matthew 6:9-13, John 17:1-26, Ephesians 1:15-21 and 3:14-21. In light of all of this, how does prayer assist us in learning to love an imperfect church? That, after all, gets to the heart of this week's study.

Prayer is like the antibiotic that fights against the viruses of envy, hate, bitterness, and other assorted spiritual ailments. No person can harbor bitterness in his heart for another and, at the same time, pray for him and not against him. Sure, there are prayers in the Psalms that speak of revenge, but that is not the way of Jesus. Prayer is like an anti-septic; it cleans up the germs that would harm us or cause harm toward another. Prayer is like a strong household product that cleans, disinfects, and deodorizes. It removes the spiritual grease and dirt that would harm our soul. Prayer can kill all spiritual bacteria. So, let's get to our exercise and start with a few questions.

1. Are you in conflict with anyone? Is there someone against whom you harbor ill-will? Has anyone hurt you recently? Is there someone in your past who continues to haunt your life, and you cannot bring yourself to ask God to bless him? Listen to what the Spirit may want to speak into your heart.

2. Name that person or those people. Speak their names aloud to God. Pray Moses's prayer for Miriam: "O God, please heal her (him) – please." Sometimes doing this little exercise of prayer will feel counterfeit or fake, but I assure you, it is not. Wise Christians have discovered that, often when we do the right actions, the right feelings will follow.
3. Speak to the Father in your own heart language. Talk with God as if He were your closest friend.
4. Confess any part that you have played in this conflict. Give some time to search your own heart.
5. Make a sacred commitment that you will go on praying for that person who hurt you until you are released from it. This could be a long journey, but one well worth the time. Most of us do not forgive in one large dose; rather, we forgive in small ingredients. Every time that person's face, or that circumstance, or that old feeling surfaces, we forgive again and again and again. Prayer is the way out of hate and the way into loving an imperfect church.

WEEK FOUR
MONDAY READING

Beyond the Borders: How do we love those who hate us?

Matthew 5:43-44

by Mike Baker

In Matthew chapter five, we come across a teaching of Jesus we call the Sermon on the Mount. It is his revolutionary teaching about the kingdom of God in which he "ups the grace ante" with his teaching on every part of life. Each word of this sermon was provocative and counter-cultural but none more so than his command to "Love your enemies!"

It was revolutionary then, and it's revolutionary now! In a world where nations hate because of borders on a map and divorced couples hate because of borders of emotion, Jesus says to love beyond the borders. In a world of friend betrayals, co-worker rumors, school gossip, and cut-throat competition, Jesus says to love those who hate us. But how?

It is important to note that, if we understand being Christ-followers from a biblical perspective, we don't hate anyone. Jesus hated no one...ever. He would have been justified had he hated the people who scourged him, the people who lied about him, the ones who mocked him while he hung on the cross, and the ones who nailed him there. But he didn't. He loved them and actually prayed for their forgiveness in the midst of his most intense human pain. If there is someone you hate right now (even if he deserves it), your prayer should focus on learning to forgive and love him as Christ did those he could've hated.

Not only did Jesus not hate, but he didn't encourage hate that already existed. He didn't adhere to the borders of separation that many in his time and culture did. He lovingly crossed borders of race, sex, social place, and religious standing. In Jesus's day, Jews didn't speak to Samaritans, but Jesus did. In his day, men didn't acknowledge women and children, but Jesus did. In his day, no one touched lepers and poor people, but Jesus did. In his day, no religious leader spent time with prostitutes and crooks, but Jesus did. As his followers, we too should live in a way that tears down the borders of enmity.

Still, we live in a world of borders and haters. Jesus says to his followers in John 15:18&19, "If the world hates you, know that it has hated me before it hated you [...] because you are not of this world [...] the world hates you." In spite of Jesus's love for all and his breaking down of barriers of hatred, he was still hated. And as this verse states, we should expect no less. Why does the world hate us? Because, as the church, we represent Him as His body and, therefore, are hated for the same reasons he was.

The world hates us for our perceived exclusivity. Because we teach as Jesus did that He is the only way to God, we are in conflict with other world religions. This may cause them to have feelings of hatred toward Christians and the church. How can we respond in love to them? Have dialogue with them that includes lots of listening and acts of kindness toward them. Focus on how Christ and His church is for everyone, including them. Don't engage in religious debates. Pray for them.

The world hates us because we represent a bad church experience. Many people in our culture are haters of all things Christian because they have been deeply hurt in the name of Christ. Many have been lied to, taken advantage of, and even abused by "so-called Christian" leaders, so naturally they hate all things associated with it. How can we respond in love? Listen to their stories of hurt and pain. Acknowledge that they were wronged. Explain that those who hurt them were not true representatives of Jesus. Apologize on behalf of the body. Point them to Christ. Ask for a second chance. Don't defend wrong actions. Pray for them.

The world hates us because we represent a standard of truth. Finally, some people hate Christ and His followers because we believe that there is absolute truth. We believe Jesus is that truth, and not to follow His ways and teachings is sin. This makes some hate us because they want to be justified in doing things their own way. They want to believe their own truth and believe it's just as good for them as any of way of life. How can we respond to them in love? Dialogue with them about their faith (everyone believes in something they can't prove). Be ready to tell them why you believe in Jesus. Tell them your

BEYOND THE BORDERS (How do we love those who hate us?)

story. Love them unconditionally. Be there when their lives fall apart.Pray for them.

None of us wants to have enemies or those who hate us, and we certainly don't want to be around them if we do. But Jesus says to love them. To do so is ridiculous. And so we are learning.

WEEK FOUR
TUESDAY READING

Beyond the Borders: How do we love those who hate us?
2 Kings 6:8-23
by J.K. Jones

I've heard people say, "Love is a verb." I couldn't agree more. It is, according to the apostle Paul: patient, kind, not envious or boastful, not arrogant or rude, not insistent, irritable, or resentful. "It does not rejoice at wrongdoing, but rejoices with the truth. Love bears all things, believes all things, hopes all things, and endures all things. Love never ends" (1 Corinthians 13:4-8). This week's video teaching from 2 Kings 6:8-23 is a reminder of love's tenacity. I know I'm not capable, apart from the indwelling Holy Spirit, to live out the kind of love that Paul describes and that the narrator of the 2 Kings 6 story unfolds through the prophet Elisha. I assume you would tell me the same thing. Even beyond that, I know, and I'm assuming you do too, that none of us are capable of loving others the way Jesus did, especially when we consider that His love was exactly the kind of love Paul described in 1 Corinthians 13. Jesus's love was always patient and kind, not envious, boastful, arrogant, rude, insistent, irritable, or resentful. Our Savior's love bears, believes, hopes, and endures anything and everything. Elisha had some of that kind of love in his heart when he chose to love his enemies, the Syrians. Let's talk about that.

The Syrians, sometimes called the Aramaeans, were a constant irritant, a prickly thorn in the side of Israel. Three of Israel's greatest kings – Saul, David, and Solomon – fought against them. Damascus was the Syrian stronghold out of which these nomadic armies attacked from the north to the south again and again. King Ben-Hadad (either Ben-Hadad I or II) was pestering Israel at the time of Elisha by sending raiding parties to steal, kill, and plunder Israelite villages. In order to understand this constant friction, it might be good to think of Syria as a playground bully. Syria ruled this little part of the world. It was never strong enough or organized enough to become a dominant civilization, but it was able to mount a reoccurring presence of hostility on God's people. Bullies are, by nature, capable of making life miserable for those they pick on and pillage. They take lunch money, routinely harass, and regularly threaten. They are joy-robbers. That's a good picture of the way Syria acted toward the northern tribes of Israel. Israel's one ace-in-the-hole was Elisha. God gave him supernatural insight into which towns the king of Syria planned to exploit. Elisha was always one step ahead of the king. It drove the Syrian king batty. He was absolutely convinced that he had a spy in his palace. So King Ben-Hadad decided that the only thing to do was to capture Elisha in the town of Dothan (6:13). Once again, Ben-Hadad was no match for Jehovah God. As the Syrian king surrounded the Dothan village, God was surrounding him with heavenly forces that the Syrians could not see. In the end, the Syrians were struck blind, and that is the exact moment when the love of God, through His prophet Elisha, revealed itself.

The Syrians were now at the mercy of the Israelites. Finally, the Isrealites had a chance to set things right. Who hasn't dreamed of punching a bully in the nose and settling old scores with a great victory? The now-vulnerable Aramaeans were led by the prophet into Samaria. At last, Israel is given the opportunity to defeat her nemesis, the bully of Palestine, decisively, to heap revenge upon a people that had made life so hard. That's when the king of Israel, Jehoram, in excitement asked twice, "Shall I strike them down? Shall I strike them down"? (6:21). Who can blame him? Elisha, though, responded in a Jesus-like fashion. Our Savior on the cross could have called down legions of angels and ended once and for all His suffering and the ridicule of the small people who mocked Him; instead, He filled that ugly six hours of pain with overwhelming grace. Elisha, like our Lord, responded with the steadfast kindness of God. He instructed Jehoram to prepare a table of food for these enemies. Instead of a great slaughter, a great feast was offered, and, to everyone's amazement, Syria no longer bullied Israel (6:23). Love is like that.

Love's capacity for making wrong things right is God's great surprise. Eugene Peterson's story of a school bully by the name of Garrison Johns reminds me of 2 Kings 6 (*The Pastor,* 46-49). Garrison picked on Eugene for sport. He ridiculed Peterson's faith and called him a "Jesus sissy." One fateful spring day, the bully caught up with the Christian. Garrison began to torment Eugene, and something snapped. Peterson discovered he was stronger than Johns. He was on top of his old nemesis, pounding away at him. Eugene asked Garrison to say "Uncle," but the bully refused. Peterson then considered his Christian training and inserted, "Say, I believe in Jesus Christ as my Lord and Savior" (48). When Johns wouldn't do it, Peterson bloodied Garrison's nose. Finally, Garrison Johns said it. Who knows, save God alone, whether that forced confession was valid or not. What I do know is that there is another way, a way that I have seen change lives over and over again. It is the Elisha way. It is the Jesus way. It is the way of the ridiculous love of the cross.

WEEK FOUR
WEDNESDAY READING

Beyond the Borders: How do we love those who hate us?

2 Kings 7:1-20

by Jim Probst

On a road trip this past spring, I read an obscure and remarkable story from the seventh chapter of 2 Kings to my family. Imagine the scene as I pleaded with our teens to unplug from the familiarity of their i-Pods in order to read an entire chapter of the Old Testament! Our SUV was littered with Chick-Fil-A and convenience store wrappers as we read a story of desperate hunger. Between sips of our 32 oz. bladder busters, we drank in a story of ridiculous love "beyond the borders."

Imagine the intensity of famine that would lead a couple of mothers to discuss which of their kids would be boiled and eaten first (see 2 Kings 6:24-33)! To be inside the gates of a city ravaged by this level of scarcity would be the second-scariest place I can think of ... the first is to be banished to the wrong side of that city's gate. This is where the lepers of the city found themselves. In good times, these suffering souls would survive on the scraps from those inside the city. But how few scraps would have been offered to these outcasts when those inside the gates were talking of eating children? In 2 Kings 7:3-4, we read of their plight and their plan: "Why are we sitting here until we die? If we say, 'Let us enter the city,' the famine is in the city, and we shall die there. And if we sit here, we die also. So now come, let us go over to the camp of the Syrians. If they spare our lives we shall live, and if they kill us we shall but die.'" Gathering their courage and strength, the four lepers set out for the enemy territory of the Syrians with a glimmer of hope for survival.

What the lepers didn't know was that Elisha had already prophesied that the famine would turn to feasting within a day (2 Kings 7:1-3). They were completely unaware that they would be used to bring good news to those who had ostracized and discarded them. Desperation drove them to pursue the improbable rather than awaiting the inevitable.

RIDICULOUS

When they had come to the outskirts of the Syrian camp, they were shocked to find the camp abandoned, "For the Lord had made the army of the Syrians hear the sound of chariots and of horses, the sound of a great army, so that they said to one another, 'Behold, the king of Israel has hired against us the kings of the Hittites and the kings of Egypt to come against us.' So they fled away in the twilight and abandoned their tents, their horses, and their donkeys, leaving the camp as it was, and fled for their lives" (2 Kings 7:6-7). This left an abundance of food, drink and valuables for the lepers to devour and stockpile. Everything the people of Samaria needed was just outside the walls they had built up around them, but they were completely unaware. The walls that were built for self-preservation became a self-imposed prison as they slowly starved.

How would you and I have responded? Would we have indulged ourselves for days or weeks before thinking of others? Would we have hoarded goods and high-fived our companions, giving little thought to those in Samaria? Even if you and I had thought of those behind the gate, would we have reciprocated the mistreatment and neglect we had received over the years?

God had clearly intervened and richly supplied this hunger-bitten troop with blessings beyond measure. Furthermore, He intended to extend this blessing through the lepers to all of Samaria. After ransacking two tents, the lepers said to one another, "We are not doing right. This day is a day of good news. If we are silent and wait until the morning light, punishment will overtake us. Now therefore come; let us go and tell the king's household" (2 Kings 7:9). While it was still night, the lepers returned to the gate with the good news of provision beyond measure. Ultimately, the prophecy was fulfilled, and the famine turned to feasting in a single day!

After reading this story to the captive audience on our road trip, I got a "thumbs up" from one of our boys and a brief conversation with all. But what does this story have to do with you and me? How are we woven into this story? Does it require more than just a nod of approval? These lepers demonstrated a kind of love that is rare in our society. I'd like to suggest that they also received a kind of love that is scarce today. On the brink of death, these lepers found life. When nearly all hope had faded, God intervened and provided more than they could ever ask for or imagine. And here's the part that stops me in my tracks … They shared the "good news" with those who would not share even proximity with them.

I've never experienced that level of rejection. I've never had to declare "unclean" when entering a city or a room. Yet, I do know what it means to be excluded from a party, a conversation, a kind gesture or an act of generosity. It stings. It hurts more than I care to reveal. In those situations, my flesh wants to lash out at those who don't love me. But that's not the love of Christ. The love I've experienced in Christ propels me to reach the unreachable. This love calls me to approach the unapproachable. It beckons me to extend love to those who clearly don't love me. It's the kind of love that the lepers demonstrated over two thousand years ago. It's the kind of love that God displayed through Christ. It's the kind of love that you and I get to convey to those who don't love us.

We have found riches just beyond the borders. We have an inexhaustible supply of everything we need in Jesus Christ. And if we are subject to our selfish nature, we'll seek to hoard it while people go hungry. But we have been changed by the love of Christ. By God's grace, we'll even take the good news to those who have rejected us, in hopes that they will not reject Christ. The famine has turned into a feast. Get the word out!

WEEK FOUR
THURSDAY READING

Beyond the Borders: How do we love those who hate us?
Ephesians 6:10-18
by Matt Fogle

"And that about wraps it up. God is strong, and he wants you
strong. So take everything the Master has set for you, well-made
weapons of the best materials. And put them to use so you will
be able to stand up to everything the Devil throws your way. This
is no afternoon athletic contest that we'll walk away from and
forget about in a couple of hours. This is for keeps, a life-or-
death fight to the finish against the Devil and all his angels. Be
prepared. You're up against far more than you can handle on
your own. Take all the help you can get, every weapon God has
issued, so that when it's all over but the shouting you'll still be
on your feet. Truth, righteousness, peace, faith, and salvation are
more than words. Learn how to apply them. You'll need them
throughout your life. God's Word is an indispensable weapon. In
the same way, prayer is essential in this ongoing warfare. Pray
hard and long. Pray for your brothers and sisters. Keep your eyes
open. Keep each other's spirits up so that no one falls behind or
drops out" (Ephesians 6:10-18 from *The Message*).

Our life as followers of Christ is for keeps, a life-or-death fight
to the finish against the Devil and all his angels. Do we really believe
this is for eternity? Gary Witherall came face to face with that question
in 2002 as a missionary in Lebanon with his wife Bonnie. Gary received
a frantic call from a friend to come quickly to the local medical clinic.
Bonnie had just been shot. When Gary arrived, he tried to get into the
room where Bonnie was being attended. Dozens of soldiers pushed him
back and eventually wrestled him down to the ground in order to keep
him from seeing his beloved wife. He was then told that a Muslim
extremist had shot and killed her.

BEYOND THE BORDERS (How do we love those who hate us?)

Gary was placed in another room in order to give him some time to absorb Bonnie's death. Anger and frustration stirred inside of him. As Gary was crying his heart out in that room, he heard a still, small voice very clearly saying, "Gary, there's a seed planted in your heart today. That seed can grow into hatred or bitterness, or it can grow into love and forgiveness. Choose!" At the memorial for his wife, he told the world press, "I forgive this man because Jesus has forgiven me." Gary, because of the ridiculous love shown to him by Jesus, chose to forgive and to show that same ridiculous love to his wife's murderer. The Gospel was preached powerfully in Lebanon and throughout the world that day because of the ridiculous love Gary shared.

Satan's tactics move in opposition to our theme of ridiculous love. He desires for us to hate, to marginalize, and to retaliate. The good news is that we can stand firm against his schemes. Our adversary is no match for our advocate and King, Jesus. We get to fight from a place of victory because of the ridiculous love Jesus demonstrated for us on the cross. While we were at our very worst, God gave us His best, so that we could experience life to the fullest (Romans 5:8).

Gary Witherall understood well who his enemy was. Do we? Do we see every day, in big and small ways, that we have the opportunity to be like Christ in loving our enemies? We have the chance to give our enemies the very best, while they are at their very worst. All of us get to extend the same ridiculous love that we have experienced with Jesus. His Holy Spirit has been placed in us today to empower us to lavish the love of God upon those in our homes, our neighborhoods, our churches, our workplaces, and on those who hate us.

Spend a couple of minutes going back through the Ephesians 6 passage. Let's allow the Word of truth to remind us who our real enemy is. Those in strategic opposition to us are not made of flesh and blood. Make some space for interceding on behalf of those who live in opposition to Jesus. Find creative ways to B.L.E.S.S. them this week. This acrostic will help us. *B*egin by praying for them. *L*isten to their stories and their needs. *E*at with them. Jesus often ate with those who were in opposition to him. *S*erve them. This is where the ridiculous love of Christ can make all the difference. *S*hare your story and the Story of Good News with them. Spiritual warfare doesn't have to lead to hate and resentment. It can be the way into authentically sharing the ridiculous love of Jesus.

WEEK FOUR
FRIDAY READING

Beyond the Borders: How do we love those who hate us?
Romans 12:14-21
by Jim Probst

Many years ago, I was on a flight home from a great mission trip. I was in that sweet spot of exhaustion and exhilaration, reminiscing about God's work in and through me. In a quick glance across the aisle, I locked eyes with a man in his late fifties who had a similar countenance about him. After a cordial "hello" and a few pleasantries, he began to tell me about his family and the son he "once had." My inquisitive look propelled him into a story of loss that had us both in tears.

This man was a pastor in a small town. On a regular study day in his office, his two boys were heading home from school on their bus route. When let off at their stop, the brothers bounded out of the bus toward home. The older crossed in front of the bus while the younger stopped in front of the bus to tie his shoe. Then … the unthinkable happened. The bus driver closed the door and lurched forward to the next drop-off, unaware of the boy hunkered down next to the front bumper. In a flash, the bus crushed the little boy to death.

Wiping the tears from my eyes, I could see that the father was eager to continue his story with an incredible mixture of grief and joy. He explained that he was only blocks from the accident and was the first to embrace the bloody little body of his baby boy. Kneeling down in the street, he was overcome with emotion and cried out to God. In a moment of sweet surrender, he began to worship God! Oblivious to what was happening around him, he sang praises to God and spoke of His character and love. As he did, the crowds gathered around in astonishment.

That very day, before the bus driver could be ridiculed, shamed, and plagued with guilt, the father sent her a bouquet of flowers with a kind note of forgiveness and grace. Instead of a lawsuit, she was offered mercy. Instead of receiving hate, she was overcome with a wave of unexpected love. The father privately and publicly expressed grace to the very woman who took the life of his son. And the people responded by the hundreds to the grace of God as He used a hope-filled funeral to draw people to Himself.

We have an opportunity to confound and compel people with the ridiculous love of God. There is much to say about the incredible man I spoke with on that memorable plane ride. We could discuss his "holy habits" of praise that bore fruit that day. We could contemplate his maturity in Christ and his responsibility to "act Christian" in his home town. But what I'd like to reflect on is his response to the one who took the life of his son. While she may not be the typical "enemy" you'd think of in this chapter, there is something in this story to inspire us toward the kind of response Paul writes of in Romans 12:14-21.

In this passage, Paul gives four negative imperatives (including positive counterparts) for addressing those who threaten us, oppose us, or cause us harm.

1. "Bless those who persecute you; bless and **do not curse them**" (vs. 14).
2. **"Repay no one evil for evil**, but give thought to do what is honorable in the sight of all" (vs. 17).
3. "Beloved, **never avenge yourselves**, but leave it to the wrath of God ... if your enemy is hungry, feed him; if he is thirsty, give him something to drink ..." (vs. 19-20).
4. **"Do not be overcome by evil**, but overcome evil with good" (vs. 21).

In many ways, I see this section of Scripture to be the playbook my fellow flier used to address the one who took the life of his precious son. I can see how he blessed rather than cursed this grief-stricken driver. I am simply inspired by how he was able to resist "repaying evil for evil" and was able to "do what is honorable in the sight of all." He also resisted any fleshly desire to "avenge himself," offering up flowers and kindness while experiencing a tidal wave of grief. Finally, evil did not win that day. Any atrocity our Enemy may have reveled in was quickly turned to victory for the countless souls who yielded to the Father in that tangible demonstration of love.

Let's bring this home to where you and I live. This section of Scripture is an astonishing assault to the "get mad and get even" mentality of our society. The very contrast highlights a kingdom value that is demonstrated best by the King Himself! Romans 5:10 reads, "For while we were enemies we were reconciled to God by the death of his Son." God the Father lead by example both then and now. He continues to beckon us to resemble Him and represent Him as we ridiculously love even those who don't love us. As you continue to wrestle with the concepts of this chapter, look for opportunities to love those that threaten, oppose, and harm you. Your reaction to their aggression might be their first glance at our Glorious God.

WEEK FOUR
SATURDAY READING

Beyond the Borders: How do we love those who hate us?

The Holy Habit of Confession

by J.K. Jones

It is spiritual-exercise-Saturday. Today's Christian discipline is confession. The primary word in the New Testament for this practice is "homologia." It literally means to "say the same thing." It involves taking what is hidden in us and declaring it publicly. In other words, there is something good and right about the practice of *confessing our sins.* Confession means to agree with what God has already said about us – that we are broken, sinful, and in need of the kind of repair that only He can give. Confession involves saying it aloud to someone. For example, when those large crowds came out to John the Baptist in the wilderness to hear him proclaim the Kingdom of God, they confessed their sins to him as they were being baptized (Matthew 3:6 and Mark 1:5).

Admittedly, there are two other kinds of confessions in the Scriptures. First, there is the kind of confession that declares *faith in Christ.* Jesus spoke of openly confessing who He was: "So everyone who acknowledges me before men, I also will acknowledge before my Father who is in heaven, but whoever denies me before men, I also will deny before my Father who is in heaven" (Matthew 10:32 and Luke 12:38). The apostle John put it like this: "Whoever confesses that Jesus is the Son of God, God abides in him, and he in God" (1 John 4:15). Paul said something similar: "...If you confess with your mouth that Jesus is Lord and believe in your heart tat God raised him from the dead, you will be saved" (Romans 10:9). So, there is confession of sins and confession of faith.

There is, also, a third kind of confession that we don't often consider. There is something we would call a *confession of praise.* Matthew 11:25 and Luke 10:21 state that Jesus *declared* (a form of *homologia)*: "I thank you, Father, Lord of heaven and earth, that you have hidden these things from the wise and understanding and revealed them to little children." So praise and thanksgiving of this kind are valid forms of confession. But what does any of that have to do with loving our enemies? For today's spiritual exercise, we want to focus on the confession of sins.

SM

The kind of confession we are talking about on this Saturday sets us free from the overwhelming burden of hiding anger, resentment, hate, and other self-destructive, sinful behavior. It is so very easy to harbor hidden grudges or to nurse old wounds. Our video teaching this week on Elisha's response to the Syrians (2 Kings 6) who wished him harm is at the heart of our exercise today. We humans hurt others and are hurt in return. If we are to love others as Jesus loved us authentically, especially our enemies, there must be a place for genuine confession. So, let's work up a holy sweat.

1. Who are your Syrians? Who has hurt you? Who has pestered and provoked you? Who, in return, have you harmed and been Syrian-like toward? Don't hurry this. Name them. Who have you thought of as an enemy? Speak that name or names aloud to God.

2. If you have a trusted friend in whom you can speak confidentially, confess to them these feelings of anger and hurt. Anger and hurt are not sinful, but can lead to sin. The real enemy, Satan, can twist them and use them to his advantage. Confession is the way out.

3. Most of us do not forgive easily or quickly. To put it in Jesus-like terms, "It is hard to bless those who curse us." It is hard to love our enemies. Spend some time reflecting on what has made this particular person or persons hard for you to forgive. Why do you continue to carry this in your heart?

4. Give careful reflection to 1 John 1:8-10. What part have we played in harboring ill will toward another? Again, there is a way out of that spiritual quick sand. It is called confession.

5. Remember that the main plot line of the entire Gospel narrative from Genesis to Revelation is God's defeat of evil and the establishment of a new heaven and a new earth. Our enemy is Satan, mortally wounded at the cross and ultimately defeated at

BEYOND THE BORDERS (How do we love those who hate us?)

Christ's final consummation. Our enemy is not the dad who may have abused us or the mother who was incapable of showing affection, or the uncle who did unspeakable things, etc. Our enemy is the devil and his forces (Ephesians 6:12ff).

6. Perhaps a prayerful reading of Proverbs 25:21-22 would help us on this Saturday's workout routine: "If your enemy is hungry, give him bread to eat, and if he is thirsty, give him water to drink, for you will heap burning coals on his head, and the Lord will reward you." Elisha would have known this. This is the very passage Paul quotes in Romans 12:20 while the insane and demonic Nero was on the throne. Don't miss this. The wise person finds in himself what he condemns in others and confesses it openly. That's how ridiculous love is shared with an enemy.

WEEK FIVE
MONDAY READING

Below the Streets: Why does the Bible tell me not to love the world?
1 John 2:15-16
by Mike Baker

In the end, they chose the tree. And why not? It was so accessible, and they were hungry. Besides, the tree offered a variety of fruit that they had never tasted before. Further still, this tree was unlike any other, located as it was in the middle of the garden with the biggest branches and most appealing fruit. Then, there was the testimony of the snake. He said that anyone who ate the fruit of this particular tree would be as smart as God and as good as God. So Adam and Eve loved the tree, ate the fruit, and lost it all!

Why does the Bible tell us not to fall in love with the world or the things of the world (I John 2:15a)? It teaches this because Satan hasn't changed his strategy much since our first created ancestors inhabited this globe. His goal is to get us to fall in love with the world because "If anyone loves the world, the love of the Father is not in him." (I John 2:15b). Jesus would later say, "No one can serve two masters, for either he will hate the one and love the other or he will be devoted to the one and despise the other." (Matthew 6:24). In other words, you have to choose who you are going to love: God or the world. It can't be both.

Enter Satan and let the seduction begin. Let's get this clear, the devil is doing everything within his power (which is limited, but strong) to make us choose the world. As we said, his strategy hasn't changed; it just manifests itself in different ways. Primarily, our enemy uses our appetite, our sight, and our pride to lure us into an adulterous relationship of loving the world. Or, as the apostle says, we are lured into "...the desires of the flesh and the desires of the eyes and the pride of life..." (I John 2:16). Let's look at each of these three.

RIDICULOUS

The desire of the flesh (our appetites). Satan will always appeal to our appetite. He does this by taking a blessing of God and making it the focal point of our existence. God made us hungry, and He made food to taste good and to satisfy our hunger. But Satan tempts us to seek the pleasure of eating, regardless of our hunger. God made us to desire intimacy, and He made sex in marriage to seal a deep friendship between a husband and a wife. But Satan has focused on the physical pleasure without the committed relationship. God made laughter to bring joy to our souls. But Satan encourages the pleasure of laughter at things that truly are hurtful. God says, "love me, and I'll give you pleasure." Satan says, "love pleasure."

The desire of the eyes (our sight). Satan also appeals to our love of beauty. He knows that we have been made in the image of God and, therefore, are made to enjoy beautiful things. God created every spectacular visual in nature and the human eyes to taken them all in. Every color you have ever seen was God's idea. Shiny, opaque, and shaded were His inventions. Texture and contour and shape came from the mind of the Creator. Our eyes are visually stimulated thousands of times a day. The devil takes this visual appeal and splashes it on sports cars, Iphone cases, clothes, video games, and much more. Subtly, he lures us in by this beauty to love the things we see instead of the One who made the colors that thrill us. In other words, we often think, "I love this red car" instead of, "I love the God who thought up the color red."

The pride of life (our pride). Finally, our adversary appeals to how much we love ourselves and want to be in charge. There is only One who deserves credit and praise and recognition for all that He has done. Yet, we also crave it. Satan manipulates this urge by making us jealous when others get credit. The devil tempts us to enjoy the words of praise and adulation others shower on us. This fallen angel once challenged God himself for the praise of heaven, so he has no problem making us believe that we too can be gods deserving of power and glory. In fact, much of our culture has an unhealthy self-esteem that is truly self worship. The Bible calls it pride, and our world has convinced many of us that our time here on earth is about "looking out for number one." The temptation is to love ourselves more than anyone or anything.

God is calling us to have a "ridiculous" non-love of the world and things in it. College students who love the Father will likely get ridiculed for not feeding the worldly appetite of drinking, sex, and thrill-seeking. Executives who love the Father more than promotions and fancy cars may get ridiculed for how out of touch they are. Church goers who love God by serving behind the scenes, without the need for recognition, may get ridiculed for being plain and boring. But this rejecting of worldly things is ridiculous only if you have not embraced the ridiculous love of Jesus. For those who have, there is nothing in this world that can compete with the love of God in Christ Jesus. As it turns out, Jesus is not only our Savior, but our example in loving God.

In the end, he chose the Father. And why not? He had the power to make stones into bread, but He was truly nourished only through relationship with the father. He clearly saw the riches of the world for what they were, cheap imitations of the glory of heaven. He knew he could have caused a spectacular scene by jumping from the temple's corner, but He lived to bring glory to God. Yes, the snake was there, telling his same old snake lies. But, in the end, Jesus loved God more than the world, and He gained it all.

WEEK FIVE
TUESDAY READING

Below the Streets: Why does the Bible tell me not to love the world?
Daniel 1:1-21
by J.K. Jones

I want to be a Jesus-follower completely in love with Him and not the world. Sunday's sermon and yesterday's reading was a reminder that ridiculous love has a cautionary side. Scripture clearly warns us not to love the world. Six hundred years before the time of Jesus, Daniel and his three godly friends understood the prohibition of not loving the world. How is that possible? The answer is rather simple. These young men understood the timeless character of God. They grasped that there was a sovereign God who loved them and had invited them into a faith-filled-relationship marked with integrity and purity. Their minds were made-up, and their hearts were resolved. All four were covenant-keepers and promise-makers. Daniel, Hananiah, Mishael, and Azariah were God-worshipers in love with their creator, but not in love with a sin-marred world. The exile and bondage that forced these four to leave Israel and to be deported to Babylon was fundamentally a result of a nation loving the world more than loving God. So, let's talk about that today.

Our choices matter. Daniel, Hananiah, Mishael, and Azariah grasped that truth. In spite of the fall of Jerusalem, in spite of the victory of Babylon over Israel, in spite of the exile from the Promised Land into a pagan culture, and in spite of all the evidence that seemed to support the conclusion that the gods of Babylon were superior to the God of Israel, there remained an unshakeable confidence on the part of these four young men in the sovereign God of the universe. Daniel and his friends were persuaded that "the Lord gave" Israel into the hands of Babylon (Daniel 1:2). King Nebuchadnezzar did not take Judah from King Jehoiakim. God alone did that. Because four fearless men believed in God, they made choices that supported their convictions. What non-world-loving choices did they make? Let me identify two.

BELOW THE STREETS (Why tell me not to love the world?)

First, they chose not to allow their name change to alter their character. The four brave-hearts of Judah chose to remain faithful to who they were. Notice with me that each of the four inherits a new name. Daniel becomes Belteshazzar, Hananiah becomes Shadrach, Mishael becomes Meshach, and Azariah becomes Abednego. Each name shift was intended to seduce and to brainwash these young men. Daniel means "God is my judge," but Belteshazzar means "Bel protects the king." Bel, obviously, is a reference to a pagan god. Hananiah means "the Lord is gracious," but Shadrach means "Aku is in command." This is another reference to a pagan god. Mishael means "Who is like the Lord?" but Meshach means, "Who is like Aku?" Lastly, Azariah means "the Lord is my helper," but Abednego means "Servant of Nego," a Babylonian god of vegetation. There is not the slightest hint in the narrative that the changing of their names shrank their faithfulness to the God of gods and the Lord of lords. Today, we are bombarded with all kinds of subtle messages that would seek to absorb our God-given identities into those of the world. The One who created us and called us into the Kingdom of light has named us His children. We are kids of the King, and our identity is found in Him. Do not love the world. What other non-world-loving choice did these four make?

Second, they chose to honor God with their everyday choices. In this specific case, they chose not to indulge in foods that the Old Testament Law clearly prohibited (Leviticus 11). We don't know the specific foods the four rejected, but what we do know is that God blessed their faith and obedience by moving favorably in the heart of those pagan leaders who were entrusted to care for all the captives (Daniel 1:9). A test was granted for ten days, and, at the end of the examination period, these brave teenagers were found to be better in appearance than everyone else who ate at Nebuchadnezzar's table (Daniel 1:15). At the end of a three year indoctrination and training season, Daniel and his buddies were found to be ten times superior in wisdom, knowledge, and understanding (Daniel 1:4 and 1:20). These four were superior to the magicians and enchanters that served at the court of the Babylonian king. Perhaps we could even say, "Ten times more in love with God." "Ten times" probably refers to completeness or beyond comparison. God took notice of their choices. He honors those who honor Him (1 Samuel 2:30). The command is clear: "Do not love the world" (1 John 2:15).

RIDICULOUS

 Choices matter. Ask William Wilberforce. His father died when young William was only nine years old, and his mother became seriously ill. Wilberforce was sent to live with an aunt and uncle who were Jesus-followers. Seeds of faith were planted in his heart, but soon he returned home and backslid into a life that embraced the world and all of its seductions. Providentially, William met several people who were marked with faith in Christ, including John Newton, the former slave trader and now apprentice to Jesus Christ. Slowly but steadily, Wilberforce became motivated by love for God and love for others, especially love for the oppressed. His long and courageous fight on the floor of the British Parliament ended slavery in the British Empire. He dared to be a Daniel and dared to stand alone. Ridiculous love is like that when it embraces the cross and not the world.

WEEK FIVE
WEDNESDAY READING

Below the Streets: Why does the Bible tell me not to love the world?
Luke 5:1-11
by Jim Probst

There are a handful of classic movies that we've introduced to our children. Among the greats is Raiders of the Lost Ark. It was quite an experience to watch this nearly-memorized film from 1981 with our kids, observing their reactions to the unfamiliar flick! You can probably recall the scene where the pilot of a little float plane is calmly fishing off one of the pontoons, nestled in the bend of a jungle river while awaiting Indy's return. Shortly after hooking a fish that turned his fishing pole into a wet noodle, the pilot heard his passenger scream from a distance, "Jacque! Start the engine! Get it up!" In just a few seconds, the inner turmoil of the pilot is visibly painful. There becomes a hilarious tension between landing the lunker or launching the plane. Jacque has to choose. He could not say "yes" to his prized pursuit and save his life and the life of Indiana Jones (who was running from an entire tribe of people who were trying to kill him). Eventually, the pole was dropped, and the rescue began.

We don't all make the wise choice in these situations. In his clever book *The Screwtape Letters*, C.S Lewis notes, "Prosperity knits a man to the World. He feels that he is 'finding his place in it,' while really it is finding its place in him. His increasing reputation, his widening circle of acquaintances, his sense of importance, the growing pressure of absorbing and agreeable work, build up in him a sense of being really at home in earth" (*Readings for Meditation and Reflection* 82). Isn't that the truth? Jacque's purpose was safely and promptly to pilot the plane. Yet, the passing of time developed a competition between his temporal hobby and his primary purpose.

Each of us has been there. We've all had to drop the pole in order to pick up the cross. Every Christ-follower experiences the death

89

of something that was once precious to him/her. From Augustine to Bonhoeffer, Theresa to Wesley, from the first converts to next Sunday's confessor of Christ, we all share the experience of a surreal surrender of the old life in light of our new life in Christ. There is nothing as perplexing as letting go of the temporal to receive the eternal. Yet that is our common Christian experience. Our purpose is to glorify God and faithfully to follow His Son while we await our homecoming. Yet, we are easily distracted by the things of this world that temporarily distract us and compete for our allegiance.

In Luke 5:1-11, we read of a call to surrender by setting aside the fish and picking up the cross. After a night of fruitless fishing, Jesus called out to the not-yet disciples to give it one more try. I'm not sure why they even bothered to listen, but in doing so, they had the catch of a lifetime. Bursting nets ushered in bursting hearts as Peter cried, "Depart from me, for I am a sinful man, O Lord" (vs.8). The next words in this incredible exchange come from Jesus to the weary and bewildered fishermen: "Do not be afraid; from now on you will be catching men" (vs. 10). The Scripture then notes that "they left everything and followed him" (vs. 11).

This is where you and I enter into the story. We are often found "fishing" when we should be "following." This world is tantalizing and alluring. Our hearts get ensnared in the trappings of temporal pursuits and distract and dissuade us from the life of a follower. "Prosperity knits a man to the World," and the clamoring and calling of every commercial compels us to forsake followership. We lay down our nets only to pick them up in a season of uncertainty, just like Peter.

After Christ's death, burial, and resurrection we see Peter resurrecting his former ways (John 21). After another long night with empty nets, Peter and the gang must have been befuddled by the words and ways of Jesus. They had seen the risen Christ twice already, but they weren't sure how to proceed in this new life. It may be helpful to re-read the John 21 account alongside the Luke 5 account. The parallels are uncanny. Ultimately, Peter laid down his net for the last time and picked up the cross-carrying life (vs. 18).

Our trappings are likely not a musty old net and a bunch of smelly fishermen. Our traps are a bit more sophisticated. We're trapped by the nets of the next promotion, the bigger house, the newer car, a slimmer physique, the admiration of a co-worker and the affection of an off-limits lover. These "nets" that we face are ensnaring to say the least. Hebrews 12:1 encourages us to "throw off everything that hinders and the sin that so easily entangles" (NIV). Perhaps we would do well to think carefully about that phrase. The three words that act like smelling salts for me are "so easily entangles." Peter was easily entangled by pursuing something of his former life. You might be "easily entangled" in one area. I might be "easily entangled" in another. Both might hinder us from a whole-hearted pursuit of followership. It's so easy.

Let's face it. A ridiculous love for Christ is incompatible with a relentless want for everything else this life has to offer. Saying "yes" to Christ is synonymously saying "no" to the nets in which we've found security and familiarity. If we are honest, we'll examine our lives and find that we are often found adding Jesus to our boat rather than going overboard to abandon ship and follow Him. Today is a new day. If you've found a familiar net in your hands and the Savior off in the distance, jump ship! Jettison the past. Swim to the shores of grace. He's eager to re-commission you.

WEEK FIVE
THURSDAY READING

Below the Streets: Why does the Bible tell me not to love the world?
Jude 17-23
by J.K. Jones

Jude, the brother of Jesus and younger son of Mary and Joseph, took great pains to remind his original readers and us of the seductive nature of the world. He wrote at a time when tolerance was more valued than truth. Does that sound familiar? Jude battles false teachers who were sexually immoral and arrogant. At the heart of Jude 17-23 is the reminder of what would happen between our Lord's first coming and His promised second coming. The apostles had spoken of this apostasy repeatedly (Acts 20:29, 1 Timothy 4:1, 2 Timothy 3:1-5, 2 Peter 3:3, etc.). Immoral, corrupt, and ungodly leaders had made their way into some of the churches. These false teachers were big on grace and short on godliness. They apparently were advocating that being saved by grace gave great freedom and license to sin, since grace covered all rebellion with immeasurable forgiveness. Think Romans 6:1: "Are we to continue in sin that grace may abound"? Like Paul, Jude gives this hearty response: "By no means"! Grace is the means to forgiveness and ushers in the necessary power to wage war against sin. It is not a license to live in a "whatever" way in a "whatever" world. Grace encourages obedience.

Note with me the words that Jude used to describe these false teachers. He called them "scoffers," "worldly people," and "devoid of the Spirit." These enemies to the Gospel pretend to know the truth but fail to live the truth. They claim deep spirituality, but the evidence points to their obvious sensuality. These divisive teachers fracture the church. The unity Christ granted us because of His finished work at the cross is harmed when these apostate leaders are allowed to go unchecked. Jude, in a brilliant move, countered this colossal mess with one word. If any of us underline words in our Bibles, this one word should be marked. It is the word "keep" (vs. 21). Jude actually uses it five times in his short letter (note verses 1, 6 – 2 times, 13, and here in this verse). The Greek word is "tereo." It primarily means to watch, to guard, or to obey carefully. The New Testament offers several examples. Prisoners were to be watched over and *kept* secured (Acts 24:23). The Sabbath was intended to be honored and *kept* with faithfulness (John 9:16). The commandments of God were to be guarded and *kept* with due diligence (Matthew 19:17 and 1 Timothy 6:14). What Jesus taught was designed to be carefully observed and *kept* and then accurately passed along to others (Matthew 28:20). This "keeping" business is intended to assist all Jesus-followers in knowing God, in enduring with a long obedience, and more than anything, in faithfully loving God and others. This kind of "keeping" is designed to ground ourselves in God's love, especially as that love relates to refusing to succumb to the world's ways.

Don't miss this one important piece. "Keep" is an imperative. Our responsibility is clear. We watch, guard, and obey in three distinctive ways according to Jude 20-21. First, we build ourselves up. This strengthening keeps us from erroneous teaching. We stay anchored by tethering our faith to the finished work of Jesus. Second, we continue praying in the Holy Spirit. We pay close to attention to the Spirit's promptings and then respond in His power and not our own. Third, we keep our eyes fixed on eternal life. That life has already begun as we have surrendered to Jesus, but it goes on with everlasting perseverance. Every single day we live in anticipation and expectation, as if this is the Day He will return. All of this causes our compassion to grow for others and lessens the hold of this world on us. The ridiculous love of Jesus awakens us to those we meet who might be seduced by these very false teachers Jude was describing.

Some of my extended family live as enemies to the cross. I find no joy in saying that. Now and then, one of my cousins will reach out and ask me to pray for some messy life situation or to do a funeral for a loved one. It is always painful. I have never refused the request. I see it as an opportunity to offer some correct teaching and to put real flesh on what the love of Jesus might look like. Several years ago, I was called to do the funeral of a baby. One of my cousins had a child that suffered from day one with health issues, and, finally incapable of overcoming the medical challenges, the baby died. The entire scenario was heart-wrenching. Friends and family members gathered. I listened to the small talk at the funeral home and graveside. So much of it centered on ungodly passions. My own story includes a battle with those same passions, but, by the grace of God, my life is under the rule and reign of Jesus. So, I simply told the Gospel story, reminded those attending the funeral that Jesus was partial to "little ones," and that His love can free us from the false love of this highly seductive world. I don't know what God will do with all of that. I only know that my love for Him and His love for me has *kept*, is *keeping*, and will *keep* me. That's what ridiculous love is like.

WEEK FIVE
FRIDAY READING

**Below the Streets: Why does the Bible tell me
not to love the world?**
1 John 5:20-21
by Jim Probst

If you were to write a note of instruction or encouragement to the church, what things would you want to emphasize? Would you talk about how often your favorite song is played, the color of the carpet, or the occasional typo in the bulletin? My guess is that you'd use the platform to share things of greater significance. But what tops the list? What does the church need to hear? With these questions in mind, turn to the book of 1 John with me.

It has been said that the book of 1 John can be summarized by the "3 Ls" of light, life, and love. The light is expressed five times, live (or walk) is used four times, and love is the dominant theme with seventeen different occurrences in this little letter to the church. It is such a powerful little statement about the priority and potency of love that we have referenced it in seven different daily writings throughout the six week study of *Ridiculous*.

If you are not familiar with how the book ends, please humor me in trying to anticipate how John concludes this masterpiece: "So now faith, hope, and love abide, these three; but the greatest of these is love"? Nope, that is 1 Corinthians 13:13: "You shall love the Lord your God with all your heart and with all your soul and with all your mind. This is the great and first commandment. And a second is like it: You shall love your neighbor as yourself"? Good guess, but that is Matthew 22:37-39. I think the answer will surprise you, as it did me.

Look carefully at the final two verses of 1 John: "And we know that the Son of God has come and has given us understanding, so that we may know him who is true; and we are in him who is true, in his Son Jesus Christ. He is the true God and eternal life" (1 John 5:20). Without too much work, we can see that we are pointed back to the central figure of our faith, hope, and love. We are reminded that the Son of God, Jesus Christ, is to be the one who has given us understanding and life itself. In fact, we are reminded twice in verse 20 that He is "true." This Greek word *alethinos* (translated as "true" in English) suggests an essence that is authentic or genuine. Jesus is the real deal!

If John's letter stopped here, it would be a great summary and a predictable ending. What stops me in my tracks is what follows. Verse 21 reads, "Little children, keep yourselves from idols" (1 John 5:21). This is a timeless truth communicated to the church of the first century and the twenty first century. Idolatry can shipwreck the light, life, and love that infiltrate this entire letter. John was concerned about the false gods that had flooded the culture and seeped into the church.

Why does the Bible tell us not to love the world? The world is filled with distractions and distortions that detract from the image of God. The "light" that is referenced five times in this letter shines brightly on the authentic and exposes the imitations. Light helps us to see the dark areas of our lives that have quietly taken the real estate of our hearts.

The "life" mentioned throughout John's writing compels us to live in a manner that is set apart for Christ, with no room for a compartmentalized faith that is relegated to Sunday morning. It is to permeate our calendar, our relationships, and our thoughts. There is no room for idolatry in this kind of life. A thorough examination of our lives will reveal much about our idols.

Finally, this "love" is to be supplied by the one who "first loved us" (1 John 4:7) and is exemplified through us to God and those He loves. Some scholars note that idolatry is closely linked to adultery. When considering the proper channels for our love, we would do well to recognize these similarities as well.

An idol is any substitute for God. It is anything that trumps our devotion to Him. Idolatry is rarely the kind of statue or "graven image" we associate with the Old Testament or foreign religions. It is more subtle, more devious and damaging than what comes to mind in a tribal ritual. Our idolatry can be disguised as child-centered parenting, pursuit of health, love of sports, retirement, or any other seemingly innocuous aspirations. Idolatry sneaks into our lives when we allow any good priority to supplant our God priority.

BELOW THE STREETS (Why tell me not to love the world?)

As you work through the discussion guide for this week, pay particular attention to the areas of your life that are sneaking up to the throne and looking for a way to topple the King. Talk with trusted friends. Examine the motives of your heart in those areas that stir your passion and pride. You may find an idol there. You may find that tomorrow's reading will equip you to remove that idol and return the King to His rightful throne.

WEEK FIVE
SATURDAY READING

Below the Streets: Why does the Bible tell me not to love the world?

The Holy Habit of Fasting

by J.K. Jones

The list of favorite Christian exercises seldom includes the discipline of fasting. I was a young security policeman stationed at McConnell Air Force Base, Wichita, Kansas back in the early 1970s. I had recently committed myself to being an apprentice of Jesus, and, with that fresh vow in hand, I had decided to cultivate the holy habit of fasting on my own. The words of Jesus in Matthew 6:16 had caught my attention: "And when you fast…" My conclusion was simple: Jesus assumed I would fast. That was enough for me. With that assumption squarely planted in my heart, I had been invited by the director of the Navigators' ministry on the base to join a group of guys in a twenty-four hour fast. I don't recall receiving much preparation. In defense of the leader, he may have guided us in readiness, but I don't remember that. What I vividly recollect is starting the fast at 6 p.m., skipping supper, doing my 8 hour shift of duty from 11 p.m. to 7 a.m., heading off-base to wash and wax my motorcycle that morning, seeing a donut shop, and, well, I broke my fast quicker than someone can dunk a glazed donut in a good cup of coffee. The end result was a pile of guilt, a bad experience, the need to confess it to the ministry leader, and an uncertainty about the value of the Christian discipline of fasting.

The Scriptures do not command Christians to fast. The Bible simply acknowledges that God-believers sometimes enter seasons where they hunger more for God and less for food. Admittedly, Israel was called to fast and to enter into an intense day of prayer once a year on the Day of Atonement (Yom Kippur – Leviticus 16:29 and 23:27). Nowhere, however, are Jesus-followers in the New Testament given an imperative to practice this spiritual exercise. So, why would we even consider it on this Saturday's reading? The answer to that important question varies. *We might choose to fast because we recognize a need for spiritual renewal.* Think of Nehemiah 9:1-2 and how Israel had returned from Babylonian captivity and needed to affirm her renewed commitment to covenant-living. *Sometimes we fast because we desire guidance and direction from God.* Consider Esther 4:16. An evil plot had been hatched by the villain Haman to kill all the Jews. Prompted by her Uncle Mordecai, Queen Esther called for a three day fast. *Perhaps we fast because a situation in the life of the church prompts a unique season of seeking God.* Think Acts 13:1-3. The Christian Church in Antioch sensed the Holy Spirit leading them to set apart Barnabas and Saul (Paul) for s special work of evangelism.

Admittedly, fasting can be dangerous. Paul warned of deceptive leaders who "require abstinence from foods that God created to be received with thanksgiving by those who believe and know the truth" (1 Timothy 4:3). Jesus cautioned against religious leaders drawing attention to their spirituality by boasting of their fasting (Luke 18:12). The truth of the matter is that we hunger for God and that He sometimes prompts us to set aside food and find our satisfaction in Him alone. On this Saturday, consider, "How does fasting assist us in not loving the world?"

Fasting is an exercise of self-denial and dependence on God. It is a Christian discipline, if it is centered on Jesus, sustained by Jesus's power, and seeks to glorify Jesus alone. Allow me to suggest *three con -* *crete ways fasting can assist us in not loving the world.* First, some believers have found legitimate motivation for fasting when they look at the poor of the world. They identify with the suffering of millions by fasting from a weekly meal in order to remember that there are those who go without food daily. We genuinely cultivate love for the most marginalized when our fast centers on the enormous suffering of so many. We practice not loving the world by not giving into its whims and temptations to think of our stomachs first. So, some of us fast a meal a week or a day a month in order to identify with the world's hungry. Second, other believers look at the continued slaughter of millions of aborted babies and find in that colossal heartbreak reason to fast once a week faithfully. Forty-plus years have come and gone since this country has legally condoned the mass killings of innocent infants caught in a culture where convenience reigns supreme. The solution to unwanted

RIDICULOUS

pregnancy is adoption, not abortion. Any country that elevates abortion diminishes love. Jesus-followers have a concrete way of not loving the world by regularly entering a day of fasting and prayer, asking God to overturn that unjust law. Third and finally, some disciples of Jesus find a legitimate reason for fasting in making a specific space for glorifying God. We fast, in this case, for our Creator and Savior to be honored. We owe our very life to Him, our salvation to Him, and our purpose in life to Him. If we want not to love the world, one of the exercises that can assist us in making Him famous is fasting for the supremacy of God. Why not start this Saturday? (See Bill Bright's *7 Basic Steps to Successful Fasting & Prayer*. Orlando, FL: New Life Publications, 1995).

WEEK SIX
MONDAY READING

Beneath the Cross: What's the big deal about the cross?
John 15:12-17
by Mike Baker

If Christ followers were asked to reduce all of their theology into a single symbol, it would likely be the cross. If a visitor from another planet came to earth (just go with it), he would notice that millions of buildings worldwide (called churches) displayed some version of the cross. Wood crosses, stone crosses, ornate simple crosses, crosses on steeples, and stained glass crosses are used to demarcate churches everywhere. Additionally, this visitor would notice that those who consider themselves Christians adorn their bodies with many representations of the cross. These artistic displays range from jewelry to tattoos and include everything in between.

This important Christian symbol is not only replicated in a variety of ways visually, but is also lyrically dominant in the musical worship of the church. Hymns like "At the cross," "There's room at the cross," and "The old rugged cross" have been sung by older generations for years. And newer generations sing "Lead me to the cross," "The wonderful cross," and "All because of the cross." Again, a total stranger would not have to experience many Sundays in a Christian place of worship before encountering the cross musically. Why so much focus on the cross? What's the big deal about the cross, especially in light of our Ridiculous study?

It was the night of his betrayal, and Jesus was just hours from hanging on this cruel form of Roman execution. His cross was two splintery pieces of wood, not gold decoration. His cross wasn't beautiful art; it was cruel torture. His cross was surrounded by mocking, not singing. But it is here, at the cross, where we gain insight into the love of Jesus as He gives some final instructions to his closest followers in John 15:12-17. In fact, the first two verses basically explain everything we need to know about the ridiculous love of Christ: "This is my commandment, that you love one another as I have loved you. Greater love has no man than this, that someone lay down his life for his friends."

The cross is the place where I was loved ridiculously. Here, Jesus expresses what all humans generally understand; the greatest form of giving is to sacrifice one's life for someone loved. We honor rescue personnel who give their lives in the line of duty as police officers and firemen. We have parades and build memorials for those who are killed defending our country in the armed forces. We call heroes those who lose their lives by stepping up to defend others in danger. To die for someone else is to love in the most ridiculous way. It is extreme. It doesn't always make sense. It is the ultimate expression. But Jesus's love is even more ridiculous.

As God, He gave his life, even though He is the giver of life. We all have people we call friends, but it's a two-way relationship. We mutually benefit from our friendships. I call you friend, and you call me friend. You are nice to me, and I'm nice to you. You give to me, and I give to you. But this is not the case with us and Christ. When he said, "I have called you friends," (John 15:15) it was a one-sided relationship. He knew we wouldn't be loyal. He knew we couldn't pay Him back. He knew that we would deny Him, forsake Him, and ultimately ignore Him. We could never give Him anything that He didn't already have. But He gave His life for us anyway. And the way in which He displayed this ridiculous love (and you and I experience it) was by His death on the cross. And this act changes the way I love.

The cross is the place where I am motivated to love ridiculously. Now that I understand how much I have been loved, what can I do but love others in the same way? Jesus begins and ends this teaching on laying down His life with a command for how His followers should respond to His great sacrifice: "This is my commandment, that you love one another as I have loved you" (John 15:12). "These things I command you, so that you will love one another" (John 15:17). I believe this was intentional because this is the why and how for my love towards others.

If Jesus loved me enough to call me friend when I was anything but, then I can befriend those who are not friendly. And if Jesus's love for me caused Him to die for our one-sided friendship, then I can love others who don't consider me a friend. Too simple? Perhaps, but think about this. Jesus isn't asking us to give the greatest love of all (laying down our lives). He's simply asking us to love with kind words, fair treatment, welcoming posture, and a willingness to see someone beyond our judgment of them. When compared to the cross, it's relativity painless. But these initial acts of ridiculous love may introduce others to the ridiculous love of Jesus.

We began by posing an improbable scenario in which a visitor from another planet witnessed all of our expressions of the cross. Some of you may have been put off by the unlikelihood of it all. But, in fact, the cross is very much about an out-of-this-world visitor who did come to earth. And becoming human, God in the form of Jesus gave His life. He became obedient to death, even death on a cross. And there, on that cross, He taught us about love, a ridiculous, undeserved, doesn't-make-any-sense, wonderful love. And when we love in this way, we are most like Him.

WEEK SIX
TUESDAY READING

Beneath the Cross: What's the big deal about the cross?
Exodus 12:1-51
by J.K. Jones

I stop now and then and remind myself of the nature of God. This seems to be a good day to do that very thing. Consider these characteristics of Him. God is worthy, holy, kind, strong, active, and just. He alone is eternal, great, creative, glorious, merciful, and all-knowing. My King is good, wonderful, present, everywhere, uncreated, and unchanging. My Lord is truthful, faithful, protective, infinite, and able to deliver and save. God is right, righteous, wise, without sin, always alert, and completely sovereign. I could go on and on. There is one attribute, though, that shapes and gives proper place to all the others, and that attribute is love. God is love (1 John 4:8). I more than recognize that God cannot be reduced or shrunk to one trait, but love does give significant definition to who He is. Love is an essential attribute of God. Some people are confused by this. They make the false assumption that God is literally defined by love. They believe God is love, and love is God. If that were literally true, we would be compelled to worship love and not God. That, of course, would run counter to everything about His supremacy. Exodus 12:1-51, from this week's video teaching, is a superb reminder of God's loving nature evident in the death of Christ on the cross as our Passover lamb. Let's give that some thought on this Tuesday.

My wife can't stand bugs or pests of any kind. On more than one occasion, I have been summoned by a scream to deal with a dangling spider, a creeping mouse, or a buzzing beetle. This Exodus story is loaded with blood, frogs, gnats, flies, livestock, boils, hail, locusts, and darkness, incredibly vivid stuff! Three rounds of intense spiritual war precede the Passover narrative. The point today, the one subject to which we want to give considerable thought, is the central requirement of a lamb. God instructed Moses and Aaron to prepare the people. On the tenth day of the first month, every family was to procure a lamb without blemish, a male a year old, and prepare it for the meal that was to take place on the fourteenth day. That gave each family nearly a week to be ready. If a family was small or couldn't afford the lamb, then neighbors were to join together and to celebrate the meal in unison. From this point on, every household would remember this particular night when the LORD passed over each home and house. Those houses marked with the blood of the lamb on the doorposts and lintels would be spared. The blood was to be a sign (Exodus 12:13). Those not covered in the lamb's blood would experience the tragic loss and death of the firstborn. That's exactly what happened. I hope you take the time to reread Exodus 12 entirely. What should not be overlooked in all of this detail is the timing mentioned in Exodus 12:29: "*At midnight* the LORD struck down all the firstborn in the land of Egypt, from the firstborn of Pharaoh who sat on his throne to the firstborn of the captive who was in the dungeon, and all the firstborn of the livestock."

This tenth and final plague took place *at midnight*. Darkness, at the stroke of twelve. Inescapable. Think about that. Recall how you feel when the power goes out in your house at night. Most of us will admit that the darkness haunts us. Our immediate action is to find that flash-light, to light all the candles we can locate, and to pray like crazy that the power comes back on quickly. Notice with me that each of the previous rounds of plagues had occurred "in the morning" (7:15, 8:20, and 9:13). Exactly 430 years had come and gone since Israel had lived in Egypt. This very night was called a "night of watching" (Exodus 12:42). Fast forward to any of the four Gospel stories. Note how three of the Gospel writers tell us that darkness covered the land as Christ, our lamb, suffered on the cross (Matthew 27:45, Mark 15:33, and Luke 23:44). John is the only one who doesn't mention this. My conviction is that he didn't have to remind his readers of darkness. John had been alluding to it all the way through his story of Jesus (1:5, 3:19, 8:12, 12:35, and 12:46). The love of Jesus Christ, like the original Passover lamb, was literally spilled out in and through the blood running down the cross, covered by the sin and shame of all of us, bathed in darkness. I can hardly see the screen on my PC because the thought of that image grabs my heart and brings tears to my eyes. More darkness, more blood, sin abounding. Ridiculous love. The perfect Lamb of God given for me and you. This Lamb protected us from the right and righteous judgment of God. I deserve to die, and so do you, forever separated from God, but He, by His love, made a way for our sins to be passed-over. The shed blood of Jesus made it eternally possible for anyone and everyone to place their trust in the finished work of Christ. The love of God, in our Savior's heart before the foundation of the world, made and makes all of this possible. It is simply ridiculous.

WEEK SIX
WEDNESDAY READING

Beneath the Cross: What's the big deal about the cross?
1 John 5:11-13
by Jim Probst

In October of 2011, I had the most eye-opening ride of my lifetime. I hadn't expected the vivid theological metaphor that unfolded as I dug my nails into the dashboard of the passenger side of a minivan. At one time in my life, I believed that the world's most aggressive driving was in Chicago. Then, I visited Peru. I thought the weaving and racing through Lima was intense until I visited Haiti. With pot holes the size of sedans and a near-hostility to traffic laws, Haiti convinced me that I thought I'd reached the pinnacle of chaos. Then, I visited India. Here, I met the Mario Andretti of India who doubles as a humble servant named Jeevan. His hospitality is legendary, and his meek and mild demeanor is simply unmatched. Everything about his disposition served and deferred to others. However, when you get Jeevan behind the wheel, he demonstrates the precision of a surgeon, the passion of a prize-fighter, and the purpose of a Great White with a maimed sea lion.

The roads are beyond crowded, and it is common to fold in the side mirrors to slip through smaller openings in the traffic. Razor thin margins and aggressive unwritten rules keep all foreigners grasping for cup holders, handles, and seat belts with great conviction. After a few shocking hours of writhing in my seat, I finally asked Jeevan how people kept from colliding with one another. It was then that the theological masterpiece unfolded.

"There are two things that need to be replaced every year," he said. "Every year we wear our brakes and our horn." While I searched for a response, Jeevan explained the complex cadence of horn usage. Demonstrating as he talked, Jevan hit the horn in various patterns and durations while explaining what each blast was indicating to other drivers. One pattern says, "I'm coming up behind you," and another says,

"I'm not bluffing; get out of my way." I was fascinated! Finally, he summarized this language lesson by gesturing toward the center of his steering wheel and saying, "This is the Horn of Salvation. No horn, no life!" This concluded the lesson.

Jeevan is a great Bible student, and he knew what he was conveying through this lesson. Jesus is known in Scripture as the "Horn of Salvation" (Luke 1:69, Psalm 18:2). And as the horn on Jeevan's minivan is absolutely essential for safe travel home through the congested streets of Delhi, Jesus is essential for life as we navigate the twists and turns of this world. John spelled this teaching out with great potency when he wrote, "**And this is the testimony, that God gave us eternal life, and this life is in his Son. Whoever has the Son has life; whoever does not have the Son of God does not have life**. I write these things to you who believe in the name of the Son of God that you may know that you have eternal life" (1 John 5:11-13).

We need to recognize that John is saying something profound, but nothing new. A quick glance at his other writing reveals a refrain that John has sung before:

> "For as the Father raises the dead and gives them life, so also the Son gives life to whom he will [...] For as the Father has life in himself, so he has granted the Son also to have life in himself" (John 5:21, 26).

> "You search the Scriptures because you think that in them you have eternal life; and it is they that bear witness about me, yet you refuse to come to me that you may have life" (John 5:40, quoting Jesus).

> "I give them eternal life, and they will never perish, and no one will snatch them out of my hand" (John 10:28, quoting Jesus).

> "Jesus said to her, 'I am the resurrection and the life. Whoever believes in me, though he die, yet shall he live'" (John 11:25).

> "And this is eternal life, that they know you the only true God, and Jesus Christ whom you have sent" (John 17:3).

BENEATH THE CROSS (What's the big deal about the cross?)

In each passage, we hear the resounding principle of this new life. It is found in Christ. This constant message is spoken to both the believer and the unbeliever alike.

For the person who has not trusted Christ unto salvation, this central message compels them to examine the lifeless choice they have made … and to respond to the message of the cross, choosing life. For those who have already trusted in Christ, the message of 1 John is a welcomed word of assurance. Here we read, "And this is the testimony, that God gave us eternal life, and this life is in his Son. Whoever has the Son has life; whoever does not have the Son of God does not have life. **I write these things to you who believe in the name of the Son of God that you may know that you have eternal life**" (1 John 5:11-13).

Why does John write "these things"? He does so that we "may **know** that we have eternal life." It is by His work on the cross that this author, giver, and sustainer of life authenticated His message, bringing victory over the grave. It is "in Him" that we are rooted, "by Him" that we love, and "for Him" that we live. "These things" are listed throughout this letter, giving indicators that we are His and becoming more like Him. Examining "these things," we find ourselves tightly tethered to the "Horn of Salvation." The road is narrow, long and winding. The way is difficult and demanding. And we are assured that we'll crash without the "Horn of Salvation." Our journey home is impossible apart from Him. But with Him comes the promise and confidence that we have life.

WEEK SIX
THURSDAY READING

Beneath the Cross: What's the big deal about the cross?
Colossians 2:13-15
by J.K. Jones

When you hear the word "trespass," what comes to mind? I vividly recall the time, about age nine, when old enough to know better, I crossed the farmer's fence-line that was clearly marked with the bold words, "No Trespassing!" I was there with a friend, who shall remain nameless, and we intended simply to stir up the cattle that were enjoying a leisurely morning of grazing. Why? I don't have the faintest clue. Boredom might be the best answer. We began to scream and make the kind of commotion that nine year old boys are capable of making, while those cows cooperated with amazing insanity. I can't recall how big the herd was, but it was large enough that it felt and sounded like a stampede. That must have been the clue to the local farmer that someone was trespassing or attempting to rustle his highly-prized livestock. He not only came out of the house in a hurry, but he came out with shotgun in hand. I kid you not. Capture the picture. The cows are already upset by our foolishness. Now the sound of buckshot filled the bizarre morning and created a picture that resembled Armageddon. The cows were running for their lives, and so were we. I had a red shirt on and thought I made a great target, so, in utter craziness, I pulled it off and tossed it to the air and kept running all the way home. The farmer must have thought enough punishment had been inflicted because my folks never heard about it, and I never went back. My cattle-stirring days were over. I would never trespass again.

Trespass is one of those slippery Bible words that often gets misunderstood. It falls into the camp of a number of other words that seek to describe the subtlety of sin. Colossians 2:13-15 uses it twice. The word is inserted some twenty-one times in the New Testament as both a verb and a noun. It paints a picture of making a false step, of

110

blundering our way across a border that is not to be crossed. It is one of those words that attempts to describe sin. In a significant passage, located in Romans 5, Paul draws on the word seven different times as he attempts to describe how death came in Adam's trespass, and life came in Christ's obedience (5:15 twice, 5:16 twice, 5:17, 18, & 20). Adam's trespass brought about condemnation and death. Christ's sacrifice on the cross ushered in justification, reconciliation, peace, grace, joy, hope, love, forgiveness, righteousness, and so much more. Adam's trespass was overcome by Christ's victory. Bible students debate whether "trespass" is a word that describes an intentional or unintentional act. In the end, it doesn't matter. Sin is still sin regardless of whether it is willful or not. What Paul was wanting to underscore with bold lines is the indisputable fact that Christ took all of our sin, the intentional kind and the unintentional kind, and tabulated all of it, took it with Him, and nailed it to the cross once and for all. Please don't miss Paul's colossal point. What Christ's act of immeasurable love did for us not only forgave all of our sin-filled debt, but freed us from that same debt. Our deliverance was won! Sin was defeated. The blood of Christ wiped away all the many sins listed on our record of debt and lay claim to all of our future rebellion. Genuine spiritual freedom was won on that defining day. Hallelujah! I mean that with all the gusto I can muster. Praise Him for what He did! Christ on the cross completely disarmed and destroyed all the spiritual powers that would lay claim over us. Christ's triumph is our triumph. Yes, we still succumb to Satan's tricks and schemes. Yes, sin is still a real part of our journey. However, in Christ, our enemy has been placed in God's great victory parade as a defeated and ultimately doomed conspirator. Our call is to live in the shadow of the cross, in the finished work of Jesus Christ once and for all. We are called to live as a forgiven and freed people. Some of us live as if Christ never went to the cross on our behalf. We live in a loveless way, a way marked by trying and trying and failing and failing. We live in fear, wondering whether we are saved or not saved. Colossians 2:13-15 and other magnificent passages like it are a strong reminder that sin's penalty and its power has been defeated through Christ at the cross. Trespasses become triumphs.

I remember how awful I felt running home shirtless and knowing that, somehow or someway, my parents would find out about my trespassing. I carried that guilt with me for months. Truthfully, I have carried worse trespasses than that in my heart for years. Now and then, a passage of Scripture will grab ahold of me, draw me in, and whisper to me of the ridiculous love of Christ. Something awakens in me. I desire to want to live as God now sees me through the finished work of His Son. I press on to know Christ and to make Him known. I carry with me His ridiculous love. Praise His name!

WEEK SIX
FRIDAY READING

Beneath the Cross: What's the big deal about the cross?
1 Corinthians 1:18-25
by Jim Probst

The message of the cross is polarizing and perplexing. Matthew's account of the crucifixion mentions there were many who derided him as they passed by the scene. The soldiers of the governor stripped him naked and gave him a crown of thorns, irreverently calling him "King of the Jews." Chief priests, scribes, and elders joined in by mocking him as well. In fact, even those who were hanging next to him were caught up in the action (Matthew 27:27-44). At a glance, the entire region slowed down only to hurl insults at a ridiculous rabbi. Jesus of Nazareth was to be pitied at best, tormented and teased at worst. Surely, this was nothing more than a delusional leader who had been deserted at the point of his greatest need.

Join me in taking a closer look as we study Luke's and John's accounts. In Luke, we see that one of the criminals has a different reaction to Jesus. This man traded ridicule for remembrance. His statement has been retold for two thousand years as one of faith and hope as he simply said, "Jesus, remember me when you come into your kingdom" (Luke 23:42). While the criminal was moved to speak, the lone disciple was speechless. John's account mentions that he was at the scene with Jesus' mother, Mary, and two other women (John 19:25-27).

I share this in order to paint this snapshot in time with vivid colors, identifying vastly different responses to the most incredible death the world would ever know. For some, this event is more of a punch line than a rescue line. In his letter to the Corinthians, Paul notes the clashing interpretations of the crucifixion and helps us to understand the basis for these differing perspectives.

"For the word of the cross is folly to those who are perishing, but to us who are being saved it is the power of God. For it is written,

'I will destroy the wisdom of the wise,
And the discernment of the discerning I will thwart.'

Where is the one who is wise? Where is the scribe? Where is the debater of this age? Has not God made foolish the wisdom of the world? For since, in the wisdom of God, the world did not know God through wisdom, it pleased God through the folly of what we preach to save those who believe. For Jews demand signs and Greeks seek wisdom, but we preach Christ crucified, a stumbling block to Jews and folly to Gentiles, but to those who are called, both Jews and Greeks, Christ the power of God and the wisdom of God. For the foolishness of God is wiser than men, and the weakness of God is stronger than men" (1 Corinthians 1:18-25).

SM Was this folly or the power of God? I trust that those reading this book wholeheartedly cling to the "Old Rugged Cross" as a moment of triumph rather than tragedy (see yesterday's reading). Paul notes a couple of fundamental flaws from those in the "folly camp."

The Jews longed for a sign while the Gentiles listened for wisdom (vs. 22). The Jews knew their Scriptures, and they were looking for fulfillment in the Messiah to come. Interpretation and anticipation had them looking in all the wrong places and overlooking Jesus. After all, how could the humble carpenter's son be the long-awaited King? Signs such as humble beginnings, a lack of military might, and death on a cross were closer to stumbling blocks than signposts to salvation in the mind of a Jew.

The Gentiles brought their own opinions to the table as well. Wisdom, in their minds, would sound a bit different than the parables that Jesus uttered. He was unconventional, controversial, and confrontational to the wisdom of the Scribes and Pharisees of the day. Some of the prophetic utterances he shared prior to the cross seemed nonsensical at best. Whether seeking a sign or wisdom, both camps seemed to miss the extraordinary power of God on display.

What is the big deal about the cross? Like the Jews and Gentiles of long ago, many of us bring our own bias and expectation to the table.

BENEATH THE CROSS (What's the big deal about the cross?)

We are looking for the King of our making rather than the King of Kings. The cross is still at the cross-roads of faith for each and every one of us. Was Jesus a victim or the victor on that dark day? Was he without sign and wisdom, or was the cross the great sign and wisdom of the Father, anticipated from the beginning of time and orchestrated flawlessly through the Savior? Paul notes that, "the foolishness of God is wiser than men, and the weakness of God is stronger than men" (1 Cor. 1:25). This kind of wisdom puts a sinless Savior on a cross to redeem the sinners writing and reading this book. This kind of strength is perfected in our weakness (2 Cor. 12:8-10). Our plan wouldn't include grace, but gumption. Our strategy wouldn't involve mercy, but might. Our plan would be rational and loveless. His plan was and is ridiculous. Don't you just love it?

WEEK SIX
SATURDAY READING

Beneath the Cross: What's the big deal about the cross?
The Holy Habit of Witnessing
by J.K. Jones

Six weeks have come and gone in this all-church-study. This is our last day to be athletes of God and to do some spiritual exercising. Today's discipline is witnessing. Think back to Mike's Sunday sermon passage from John 15:12-17. In that Scripture, Jesus said, "This is my commandment, that you love one another as I have loved you. Greater love has no one than this, that someone lay down his love for his friends. You are my friends if you do what I command you [...] These things I command you, so that you will love one another." Remember that these words are spoken in the borrowed Jerusalem Upper Room where Jesus celebrated the Passover with His inner circle. He would soon experience betrayal, desertion, persecution, and death. All of His words are pointing toward the cross. In essence, Jesus was offering His finest proof of love. He foresaw the arrest in Gethsemane, the subsequent illegal trial, and His willingness to surrender His life on behalf of the sin of the world. Jesus does what John 15:13 portrays. He laid down His life for us. Ready or not, that same kind of self-emptying love is to be the sort of love that all Jesus-followers are to show toward one another. What does all of that have to do with the discipline of witnessing?

Jesus had reminded His disciples earlier, and now reminds us, that our love for one another would be the avenue through which people would know that we are in relationship with Him (John 13:34-35). I can't speak for you, but I know my deepest need is for more love. I need all the love that Christ can bring to bear on my life. I need all the love that Christ can give me in order to offer that same love to those who are in apprenticeship with Him. I need all the love that Christ can give me in order to reciprocate that same love with those who have not yet met Him. I don't know of anything that I need more than the love of Jesus

116

BENEATH THE CROSS (What's the big deal about the cross?)

Christ. Without exception, all of us need that love. Witnessing, at its
very core, is simply sharing the love of Christ with those around us that
we ourselves have already experienced from Him. We witness to His
love on the cross. We witness to the change His love has made in us. We
witness to His love by indiscriminately sharing His story and His love
with those we meet. Our fundamental desire is to love the way Jesus
loved and loves, right?

1. So, here are some practical suggestions for today's exercise:
2. Pray for an opportunity to love someone in Jesus's name today.
3. Pay attention to how the Holy Spirit brings someone into your
   path.
4. Be practical and not theoretical. Who needs help around you?
   Does a neighbor need assistance? Does a yard need mowed,
   raked, or weeded? Does someone's car need washed? Is a gro-
   cery store-run for a needy neighbor required? Look around. If an
   opportunity surfaces, tell the person or family why you are willing to serve.
5. If the day allows for it, simply sit outside. Greet anyone who
   walks by. See if the Holy Spirit gives you an opportunity to
   engage that person in conversation.
6. Just speak the name of Jesus. If further conversation ensues,
   press on.
7. We make witnessing too hard. Witnessing is simply demonstrating and testifying to the love of Jesus. We don't have to do
   everything or tell everything in one setting. The whole Gospel
   story is not required in most situations.

Phil Ryken, in his remarkable book *Loving the Way Jesus Loves*,
tells the story of Kim Phuc, the nine-year-old girl made famous by a
photograph from the Vietnam War. Kim was the terrified and naked
child running away from a napalm attack outside Saigon, now called Ho
Chi Minh City. The date was June 8, 1972. She recalled seeing the low-
flying airplane coming toward her with bombs falling everywhere. Her
clothes had been burned off by the napalm fire. An American soldier
came to her aid, offering her a drink, while pouring water over her body.
Kim spent fourteen months in the hospital and endured seventeen opera-
tions. She testifies today to how her family lost everything – home,

clothes, and resources. Her anger boiled inside of her. She hated her life. As the days methodically went by, Kim found herself spending time in the library and reading religious books. One of the books that providentially made its way into her life was the Bible. Christmas, 1982, ten-plus years after the horror of the napalm attack, she accepted Jesus Christ as her personal Savior. God instantly entered her life, and the hate that lived there for all those years miraculously began to exit. God empowered her to forgive. The love of Christ was making its way into every part of Kim's life. Her testimony is powerful: "Forgiveness made me free from hatred. I still have many scars on my body and severe pain most days, but my heart is cleansed. Napalm is very powerful, but faith, forgiveness and love are much more powerful" (174). Kim Phuc's testimony is clear: we witness to the ridiculous love of Jesus that we ourselves have experienced. Praise the Lord for His unchanging love. Share it today.

STUDY GUIDE
HOW TO USE THIS STUDY GUIDE

Thank you for your willingness to participate in this study! We pray that this material will work its way into the lives of thousands of participants in hundreds of small groups. This study is designed to synthesize a variety of resources in various venues over the next six weeks. There are also age-specific discussion points for a wide range of participants. You will notice three distinct icons in the margin of the daily readings. Each icon will draw your attention to specific segments of the writing as you prepare to discuss key concepts in each study.

▶ **College Ministry**

🏠 **Family Ministry**

🆂🅼 **Student Ministry**

Throughout this study guide, we will be challenged by the following material:

- Daily reading for personal reflection

- Weekly video teaching and discussion for group interaction and accountability

- Weekend church services that reinforce the weekly themes

- Occasional action points to help mobilize groups and individuals to apply lessons learned

In order to get the most out of this study, please commit to the daily reading in this book and review each week's discussion guide prior to meeting as a group. Here, you will see each week's discussion framed by three main sections:

- Summarize: Capture the key components of the daily reading and the video teaching

- Discuss (Personalize): Examine the ways in which the stories from Scripture intersect with our own stories

- Mobilize: Engage in practices that turn our reflections into actions

We are confident that God will use this resource to reveal great things about His nature and the way that He is calling you to be more like Christ. Furthermore, your thoughtful participation in personal reading and group interaction will inspire others to grow to be more "ridiculous" as well.

In Christ,
Jim Probst
Pastor of Small Groups
Eastview Christian Church
www.eastviewchurch.net

WEEK ONE
BEFORE WE BLEW IT
(What is God really like?)

---

1 John 4:19 declares, "We love because he first loved us." In this chapter, we explore the initiating and inspiring love of God. A study through five passages and the practice of one "spiritual discipline" will help us to reflect on the character of the Father and to respond as His children.

KEY QUOTES FROM THE VIDEO TEACHING

- "Smedes made this statement: he said, 'the deepest motive for believing is the awareness of being loved by God.' If there is a character in the Old Testament who stretches that almost to the point of braking, it is King Manasseh." –J.K. Jones

- "It is in Ephesians chapter 1 verse 4 where Paul says, 'he chose us in him before the foundation of the world.' King Manasseh tests that." –J.K. Jones

- "This king is an extraordinary example of wickedness, set alongside the unfathomable love of God. I can't wait for us to explore this." –J.K. Jones

- "... All the good stuff that we want to do and all the good stuff that we want to be begins in the personality of God." –Mike Baker

- "If I am going to love you in a ridiculous way, if I am going to love my wife in a ridiculous way, if I am going to love people who don't like me in a ridiculous way, then somehow I am going to have to tap into that reality of God's love. Because only God understands how to love somebody when He doesn't have to." –Mike Baker

KEY QUOTES FROM THE DAILY READING

- "In essence, the entire story of mankind is God's continual display of love for us. He sought a love relationship in the garden with our parents, Adam and Eve. He sought a love relationship through covenant with our father Abraham. He sent love letter after love letter through his prophets, calling His people back into loving relationship with Him. But His ultimate display of love came with a gift of inestimable value when God wrote a letter in the person of his son, Jesus." –Mike Baker, Monday's reading.

- Regarding King Manasseh, "His encounter with the living God caused Manasseh to work at reversing his previous years of apostasy. Maybe your story is just like that. The incredible love of God has a way of recalculating our life's direction." –J.K. Jones, Tuesday's reading.

- "Jimmy didn't know the ridiculous love of the Father. He was wrapped up in the world's narrative of earning approval and being 'good enough' to be loved. That kept him on the outside, looking in. He had not heard this message of God's love. He had only heard of God's disapproval, disappointment, and disregard for those who have made bad choices. That narrative is so consistently and loudly chanted in our society that it is hard to hear the sweet sound of the Father." –Jim Probst, Wednesday's reading.

- "We are a people hungry for love but gorging ourselves on lesser foods. God's love is the deepest nourishment that we can give our souls, but we often struggle to believe that God even likes us. After blowing it in the Garden, we have forgotten what God is really like." –Charlie Welke, Thursday's reading.

- "It is important to understand that the Father's love is demonstrated, not in a void, but in full knowledge of our sin. The reality that 'we blew it' did not give the Father an escape clause in His holy contract with us. He continued to pursue us and to provide for us in our times of deepest need." –Jim Probst, Friday's reading.

• Speaking of the spiritual discipline of meditation, J.K. Jones notes, "we are filling the mind with Scripture and not emptying it. With that said, let's practice the holy habit of Christian meditation." –Saturday reading.

PART TWO: DISCUSS

PERSONALIZE YOUR DISCUSSION STARTER

Choose one of the following to engage your group in discussion:

• Describe your first home as an adult.
• As a group, name as many famous fathers as you can in two minutes. Do they tend to be positive or negative examples? Explain.

DIG IN DEEPER

1. Invite someone in the group to begin the study by leading the group in prayer.

2. Watch the video for week one, "Before We Blew It: What is God really like?"

3. Did anything surprise or inspire you in this week's video? Explain.

4. Read the quotes from the video teaching.

5. The third quote from the video teaching highlights the contrast between a wicked king and a loving Father. Does this challenge your thinking about forgiveness and love? Does it confirm anything for you?

6 What Scripture reference or daily reading did you find most helpful this week? Explain.

7 We will address "ridiculous" love from various perspectives throughout this study. Before we move from "personalizing" to "mobilizing," take a minute to write one sentence that summarizes the impact of this week's teaching for you. Share your sentence with the group.

PART THREE: MOBILIZE

1 As we heard in the video teaching, we may be motivated to make some changes in our thoughts and behaviors this week. However, don't skip to action too quickly. Take time to marvel at the Father's love for us.

- Re-read Saturday's daily reading. Look for ways to meditate on the Scriptures provided.
- Journal about the concepts that most impacted you this week.
- Look for opportunities to share what you are discovering with a trusted friend.

2 Share prayer requests with the group, inviting someone to take notes and to email the requests to the entire group after the meeting.

3 Continue with your daily readings and review next week's study guide, entitled "Behind Closed Doors (Is it possible to love my family the way God loves me?)."?

FAMILY GUIDE

Throughout the next 6 weeks, we pray that you will use this study guide to create teachable moments with your children. Strategically set up times for your family to read the Family Focus Verse, lead an age-appropriate discussion on how this applies to our lives, and pray together as a family.

FAMILY FOCUS VERSE

1 John 4:19
"We love God, because He first loved us."

FAMILY FAITH DISCUSSIONS

- Gather all the kids into one of the bedrooms at bedtime some night this week.
- Briefly tell them a G-rated version of Manasseh's story and how God's love shows up in that story.
- Make sure you teach your kids (no matter their age!) that God loves them even though they have sinned. Like Manasseh, He loves us into a changed life.
- Take time to pray together as a family – each person saying something they love about God. Close by thanking God for loving your family before you all loved Him.
- Taking our cue from Saturday's reading, encourage your kids to fall asleep thinking about how wonderful God is.

Keep it short. Keep it simple. Keep it real.

STUDENT MINISTRY PARENT GUIDE

BIG IDEA

In Friday's reading it explains, "God's love for us was eternally established 'before we blew it' by our sin, but not blissful ignorance of our sin...'while we were still sinners, Christ died for us' (Romans 5:8)." Your student needs to know that even when they blow it, you will always receive them back with both mercy and discipline—not condemnation or complete dismissal. They take their cues on God's character from what they see modeled from you.

DAILY REFLECTIONS

- **Monday:** "Each of us holds a deep desire to love and be loved." Now that your son or daughter is a teenager and likely feeling the buzz to date, what is one practical way that you can begin showing them what real love looks like? What questions could you start asking to help them come up with the wise and Godly conclusion?

- **Thursday:** "We are a people hungry for love, but gorging ourselves on lesser foods. God's love is the deepest nourishment that we can give our souls, but we often struggle to believe that God even likes us." Whether you have a 6th grade girl or a senior boy, your student is wrestling inside with their worth and identity. It may feel awkward on your part, but what is something you could do this week to affirm your son or daughter in their identity in Christ? Even if it isn't seemingly well received, know that your approval means more than anyone's to them deep down.

WEEKLY DISCIPLINE

- **Saturday:** Meditate–As you meditate on 1 John 4:19 this week, let the truth that you are God's beloved remind you who you are. Love for your student will flow out as a response in the form of affirmation and patience to really listen to their heart. Say a prayer before you reciprocate a poor attitude they might be having.

CAMPUS MINISTRY GUIDE

DAILY REFLECTIONS

Look back at the first quote from the daily readings – how does what Mike said on Monday about God's ridiculous love shape our reading of Scripture?

- **Tuesday:** After hearing the transformational story of Dawson Trotman, what type of power is there in the simple question, "Do you like this kind of life?" How might this question be one of the most revealing in the life of a college student?
- **Friday:** What does the alternative writing of John 3.16 at the outset of the chapter make you think? How have you seen this perception of God on your campus?
- **Saturday:** Meditation = "filling the mind with the Word of God" – how might filling your mind with the messages of God's ridiculous love change your perception of yourself, your campus, and your time in college?

WEEK TWO
BEHIND CLOSED DOORS
(Is it possible to love my family the way God loves me?)

PART ONE: SUMMARIZE

1 John 4:7 reads, "Beloved, let us love one another, for love is from God, and whoever loves has been born of God and knows God." As we study these passages, apply practical teaching, and practice the "discipline" of "examine," we look to emulate the "ridiculous" love of God in one of the most neglected and underestimated segments of our society … the home.

KEY QUOTES FROM THE VIDEO TEACHING

- "And David said, 'Mephibosheth!' And he answered, 'Behold, I am your servant.' And David said to him, 'Do not fear, for I will show you kindness for the sake of your father Jonathan, and I will restore to you all the land of Saul your father, and you shall eat at my table always.' And he paid homage and said, "What is your servant, that you should show regard for a dead dog such as I?" –Mike Baker, quoting 2 Samuel 9:1-8

- "Here's a king, a powerful king, and the amazing thought that comes to his mind is, 'how can I love on the former king's family,' the king who tried to kill King David. And what is so remarkable about that response historically is that kings typically conducted a brutal purge in the early part of their rule and reign, and they killed all potential threats to the throne." –Mike Baker

- "There is perhaps not a greater laboratory for living out ridiculous love than the family table [...] that is one of the most formative places for ridiculous love." –J.K. Jones

- "What amazes me is that he invited him to the king's table. The most intimate place of fellowship, the place of families where laughter happens, it's where life happens, it's where conversation [...] for a king it would be a place where he sat around with his sons and his generals and all the people who were important, planning stuff for the kingdom and wars and strategies." –Mike Baker

- "It is really behind the closed doors where we find ourselves going, 'Okay, I'm either going to live like God wants me to live, and I'm going to love you, or I'm not.' And, you know, even John goes on to say, 'if you can't love your brothers, then you can't love God.'" –Mike Baker

KEY QUOTES FROM THE DAILY READING

- "Well, our teaching from 1 John is about a family trait that identifies all believers as members of God's family. Genetically speaking, members of this family vary greatly in their appearances, but, spiritually, we are unmistakably identified by the love we share with one another." –Mike Baker, Monday's reading.

- "Every time we share in the Lord's Supper together, we are reminded that our King invites each of us, crippled and broken by sin, to dine with Him. Talk about ridiculous love!" –J.K. Jones, Tuesday's reading.

- "Once again, let's look at the picture that is painted by the faithful marriage of a husband and wife. Those covenant-keeping men and women point beyond their marriages to the marriage described in Revelation [...] This submission, love, and respect is a harbinger of a wedding and marriage beyond our wildest dreams." –Jim Probst, Wednesday's reading.

- "This idea of living our lives with ridiculous love cannot merely be a façade for the public portion of our lives. It cannot be like a nice outfit we put on when we want to look good and take off when we want to feel comfortable. It becomes who we are and shows up where we are." –Jason Smith, Thursday's reading.

- "In a society that is increasingly individualistic, this 'membership' is often dismissed or minimized. Yet, God designed us for profound interdependence. Our families can be the training grounds for a 'we' mentality in a 'me' world." –Jim Probst, Friday's reading.

- "Self-examination is at the very center of a healthy relationship with Jesus. This exercise is not some morbid introspection […] Rather, this specific discipline is the mark of someone who desires to cooperate with God's intention to grow to look more and more like Jesus." –J.K. Jones, Saturday reading.

PART TWO: DISCUSS

PERSONALIZE YOUR DISCUSSION STARTER

Choose one of the following to engage your group in discussion:

- Describe a common childhood dining experience with your family. Where was it? Who was there? What typically took place during the meal?
- As a group, discuss some of the most memorable dining experiences of your lifetime. Was it the place, the people, or the food that made it so memorable?

DIG IN DEEPER

❶ Take a moment to read the "summarize" section of this week's study.

2 Invite someone in the group to begin the study by leading the group in prayer.

3 Watch the video for week two, "Behind Closed Doors: Is it possible to love my family the way God loves me?"

4 Did you take any notes during this week's video? What concepts were worth noting?

5 How does the story of Mephibosheth parallel the ongoing invitation for Christians to participate in communion?

6 Read the quote from Friday's reading. In what way has the family helped you to understand interdependence?

7 What Scripture reference or daily reading did you find most helpful this week? Are there other passages that are helpful as we think about this topic? Explain.

8 As you think about your current family situation, do you find it to be more or less Christ-centered than what you experienced in your childhood? Explain.

PART THREE: MOBILIZE

1 In response to the video teaching and this discussion, we may be motivated to examine our family environment this week. Take time to evaluate the level of love demonstrated with those closest to you. Is it ridiculous?

- Re-read Saturday's daily reading. Look for ways to practice examination this week.
- Write and deliver a "love letter" to at least one family member this week.
- Look for opportunities to share what you are discovering with a trusted friend.

2 Share prayer requests with the group, inviting someone to take notes and to email the requests to the entire group after the meeting. Try to narrow the focus to your own demonstration of "ridiculous love" this week.

3 Continue with your daily readings and review next week's study guide, entitled "Between the Pews: How do I love an imperfect church?"

FAMILY GUIDE

FAMILY FOCUS VERSE

1st John 4:21
"Whoever loves God, must also love his brother."

FAMILY FAITH DISCUSSIONS

- This week, cook (or order in) some of your kids favorite foods and have a special family night.
- At dinner, tell the story of Mephibosheth and the king's dinner table to your kids. Briefly talk to them about something that touched your life in this week's study.
- Ask your kids what type of family you want to be (sharing, kind words, serving, etc.).

Write their ideas on something you can keep displayed: Our family is…

- Pray as a family, asking God to help you become the family you described in your discussion. Put your visual somewhere where everyone will see it often.

Keep it short. Keep it simple. Keep it real.

STUDENT MINISTRY PARENT GUIDE

BIG IDEA

Monday's reading centers us on that fact that often, our comfort level and our history—both the good and the bad, often make it difficult for us to love our families as God loves us. Even as your teenagers have attitudes, seem ungrateful, and are gradually pulling away, they all still desire a place to belong and be accepted. They need help navigating the deep waters of adolescence and need you as their guide.

DAILY REFLECTIONS

• **Tuesday:** "In both the Old and New Testament, the dinner table takes on significant, God-centered meaning." What does family time look like in your house? Is it a sacred rhythm or easily interrupted or skipped? What would it look like for you to make a weekly ritual of family time that your teenager was required to attend? Make it something they would enjoy being a part of—whether that is dinnertime around the kitchen table, or a few rounds of "Just Dance" and a bowl of ice cream.

• **Wednesday:** "The metaphor of a covenant relationship between Christ and his church is on display in Christ-centered marriages." Take a few moments to examine the temperature of your marriage. When was the last time you had a date night-even if just for an hour or two? In what tone are words spoken, or under what attitudes are acts of service performed? Your students are watching. The way you love each other makes them feel loved as a by-product. They will learn what ridiculous love looks like by seeing it in your marriage.

WEEKLY DISCIPLINE

• **Saturday:** What would be a good rhythm be for you to examine the question JK gave: "Did my family see God in me today?"

CAMPUS MINISTRY GUIDE

DAILY REFLECTIONS

The paragraph noted in Monday's reading addresses a struggle that many college students face. Before diving into the questions this week, spend some time reflecting and sharing on what kind of family narrative you are a part of.

- **Thursday:** Recognizing that "sacrifice of self" is the key to a flourishing family life, in what ways have I seen members of my family exhibit this truth? In what ways have I seen the contrary?
- **Friday:** How do college students tend to project a "me-centered" attitude within their families? Why might college be a time in life that we are more susceptible to this temptation?
- **Saturday:** Self-examination = "mark of someone who desires to cooperate with God's intention to grow" – what is being revealed about us as we examine ourselves in light of Christ's ridiculous love for our family?

WEEK THREE
BETWEEN THE PEWS
(How do I love an imperfect church?)

PART ONE: SUMMARIZE

John 13:35 reads, "By this all people will know that you are my disciples, if you have love for one another." In the best of environments, it is difficult to love one another "ridiculously" . In an imperfect church (filled with imperfect people), we have the opportunity and responsibility to love one another in such a way that our faith is authenticated by those observing us.

KEY QUOTES FROM THE VIDEO TEACHING

- "Moses is the leader of God's people. But Moses had this deal where he went out frequently to the tent of meeting where God would speak to him as a man speaks to his friend. And so Moses is the leader, but Miriam and Aaron are comfortable enough with him to start criticizing him." –Mike Baker

- "I just want to share briefly from this passage three ridiculous love killers that were in this story and are also true in the church today. And the first one is judging other people." –Mike Baker

- "That leads to this other love killer in the church, and that's jealousy [...] Miriam and Aaron were jealous of Moses [...] it occurs to me that they were a little miffed because it seemed that Moses was getting all the glory [...] he was getting famous as the leader of God's people." –Mike Baker

- "And then finally is the word 'gossip.' I don't know if you picked up on this or not, but in verse 1 Miriam and Aaron spoke against

Moses. It's so easy to talk to other people about the weaknesses you see […] The bottom line is that God encourages us not to talk about one another but to talk to one another." –Mike Baker

• "It goes all the way back to Adam and Eve and their sin. God was very gracious to them and loving to them, and he told them not to do one thing, and they did it anyway." –Mike Baker

KEY QUOTES FROM THE DAILY READING

• "We love imperfect people by constantly reminding ourselves how God has loved us in Christ […] I'm not sure we can answer how He could love us. But He does. So we can try to offer to others what we have received so freely." –Mike Baker, Monday's reading.

• "Time and time again, Moses pleads to God, on behalf of Israel, not to destroy His people. That loving heart is the very one that makes the difference in the insurrection of Aaron and Miriam toward Moses; I implore you not to miss this. In Moses' words to God, on behalf of Miriam, is the secret of a loving heart: "O God, please heal her — please" (Numbers 12:13). She doesn't deserve it. She can't earn it. Moses freely gives it. Why? The answer is clear. God had transplanted His heart into Moses. That same God is able to do the needed surgery on you and me." –J.K. Jones, Tuesday's reading.

• "Every great leader takes people on a journey rather than telling them where to go. In other words, leaders concern themselves with moral authority more than positional authority. The Apostle Paul's charge to 'Be imitators of me, as I am of Christ' comes to mind (1 Cor. 11:1). When we think of the great expectations that Christ has for us, we can be confident that they were preceded by great examples. Here in 1 John 3:16, we are reminded that the standard of loving others is set by Jesus as He 'laid down his life for us.' His example is the basis for our imitation. We are not simply encouraged to appreciate His sacrifice for us, but to emulate it." –Jim Probst, Wednesday's reading.

- "This new commandment from John 13 is of the utmost importance. I love that this commandment to love one another well is sandwiched in John 13 between Jesus telling his disciples that He will be betrayed by one of them and telling Peter that He's going to be denied by him. The structure of John 13 preaches to me a lot." –Caleb Baker, Thursday's reading.

- "I don't think God is surprised by the difficulties of community. I think it is the crucible He uses for shaping and refining us. God, in His wisdom, designed us to be in community. His call for us to be authentic is not at odds with the reality of our imperfection. He pulls together all of our dysfunction, warts, and shortfalls, and He calls us His bride (see Eph. 5:22-33)." –Jim Probst, Friday's reading.

- "Prayer is like an antiseptic; it cleans up the germs that would harm us or cause harm toward another. Prayer is like a strong household product that cleans, disinfects, and deodorizes. It removes the spiritual grease and dirt that would harm our soul. Prayer can kill all spiritual bacteria." –J.K. Jones, Saturday reading.

PART TWO: DISCUSS

PERSONALIZE YOUR DISCUSSION STARTER

Choose one of the following to engage your group in discussion:

- Some people thrive in clutter and chaos. Others do best with a high degree of control and order. Which end of the spectrum best describes you? Explain.
- In your opinion, is it easier to "love an imperfect church" when the church attendance is a few hundred or a few thousand? Explain.

DIG IN DEEPER

1. Invite someone in the group to begin the study by leading the group in prayer.

2. Watch the video for week three, "Between the Pews: How do I love an imperfect church?"

3. Read the notes from this week's video. Is there anything from the story of Moses, Miriam, and Aaron that you've experienced in the church today? Explain (without naming the church or the individuals associated with the situation).

4. Review the quote from Wednesday's reading. How have you observed faithful leadership in the church?

5. Read the quote from Thursday's reading. Consider the structure of John 13 and the context of Jesus's call to love one another. Share your insights with the group.

6. How does the quote from Friday's reading reflect the teaching from John 13? Explain.

7. If church health is measured by the way in which we love one another, has our church passed her physical? Explain.

8. Are there any additional Scripture references or insights from the reading that may be helpful at this time?

PART THREE: MOBILIZE

1. There are many thought-provoking questions left at the conclusion of this Saturday's reading. Take time throughout this week to respond to these helpful prayer activities:

- Are you in conflict with anyone? Listen to what the Spirit may want to speak into your heart.
- Name that person or those people with whom you remain in conflict. Speak their names aloud to God. Pray Moses's prayer for Miriam: "O God, please heal her [or him] – please." Sometimes doing this little exercise of prayer will feel counterfeit or fake, but I assure you, it is not. Wise Christians have discovered that, often when we do the right actions, the right feelings will follow.
- Confess any part you have played in this conflict.
- Make a sacred commitment that you will go on praying for that person who hurt you until you are released from it. This could be a long journey, but it will be one well worth the time.
- Look for opportunities to share what you are discovering with a trusted friend.

2 As a group, commit to pray daily for the leaders of the church. Decide whether to continue this prayer initiative throughout the rest of the week or the rest of this study.

3 Share prayer requests with the group, inviting someone to take notes and to email the requests to the entire group after the meeting. Try to narrow the focus to your own demonstration of "ridiculous love" this week. In particular, look for ways to pursue unity and love within the church family.

4 Continue with your daily readings and review next week's study guide, entitled "Beyond the Borders: How do we love those who hate us?"

FAMILY GUIDE

FAMILY FOCUS VERSE

John 13:35
"By this all people will know that you are my disciples,
if you have love for one another."

FAMILY FAITH DISCUSSIONS

- This week, take a natural time in your schedule and have a snack with your family at church – perhaps right after services would work best.
- Discuss the things everyone likes about being a part of this church.
- Ask the kids about their friends that they have at church and what makes it cool to be with those friends.
- Gently ask if there are people in the church that your kids don't like very much or have a hard time getting along with.
- Read John 13:35 from one of the kids' bibles and talk to them about how our love for our Christian friends sends a special message to those who don't know Jesus yet.
- Close your time by having everyone pray for one friend and for one person they have trouble loving.

Keep it short. Keep it simple. Keep it real.

STUDENT MINISTRY PARENT GUIDE

BIG IDEA

In Monday's reading it says that we can "love imperfect people by constantly reminding ourselves how God has loved us in Christ." Even though your student(s) may be imperfect, the perfect love of God can empower you to love them ridiculously.

DAILY REFLECTIONS

• **Wednesday:** "Every great leader takes people on a journey rather than telling them where to go... When we think of the great expectations that Christ has for us, we can be confident that they were preceded by great examples." How often do you tell your kids to obey you just because you said so? How often can you say you're telling them to obey because you're setting the Christ-like example in and out of your home?

• **Thursday:** "the type of love we have for one another within our church family shouldn't look like the rest of the world; it should raise some eyebrows." How have you loved your imperfect family this past week in ways that would raise some eyebrows?

WEEKLY DISCIPLINE

• **Saturday:** Prayer – How might you go about intentionally praying for your kid this week? Ask them what you can be praying for this week and set aside a few minutes a day to get on your knees before God and lift up your kids.

CAMPUS MINISTRY GUIDE

DAILY REFLECTIONS

College students have become well-versed in creating reasons to "not" love the Church. Many of those reasons are addressed in Mike's "how" question line in Monday's reading. Why is it especially important that a Jesus-follower cultivate reasons to love the Church while in college?

- **Wednesday:** In what ways and places have I seen or heard the wounds, disappointments and criticisms of the Church on campus?
- **Friday:** What would a group of students on the campuses look like if they exemplified the things described in Biblical community? What type of impact could this type of fellowship have on the campus at large?
- **Saturday:** Prayer = "Jesus follower's essential ingredient" – utilize the summary list marked in the chapter and pray one of those prayers each day for the upcoming week.

WEEK FOUR
BEYOND THE BORDERS
(How do we love those who hate us?)

PART ONE: SUMMARIZE

In Matthew 5:44, Jesus says, "But I say to you, love your enemies and pray for those who persecute you." As Christians, it is not "us vs. them," but "us for them." We are challenged throughout the Scriptures to demonstrate love for those who have no love for us!

KEY QUOTES FROM THE VIDEO TEACHING

- In reference to 2 Kings 6,"this is one of the most radical teachings of Christianity. I mean, it separates it from any other world religions or world teaching or worldview that you should love people who don't like you." –Mike Baker

- "And Elisha prays […] that the eyes of the servant are opened […] and he's allowed to see that […] the hills are filled with horses and chariots of fire. The army of the Lord is on their side." –Mike Baker

- "I have to mention here that, through Jesus Christ, 1 Corinthians 15:26 and then 54-57 mentions that we have been delivered from our two greatest enemies, from sin and death, because of the death, burial, and resurrection of Jesus Christ. So God has a pattern of delivering from enemies." –Mike Baker

- "Here're some rules to follow for you and I when enemies come into our life, when they attack us. Here's the first one: don't seek vengeance."

- "Behind every study that we're doing in this 'ridiculous' focus is the idea that God's love gives shape to all other kinds of love. So I want to come back to that predominant idea. Are you telling us that God's love compels us, I chose that verb intentionally, compels us to love our enemies?" –J.K. Jones

KEY QUOTES FROM THE DAILY READING

- "It is His revolutionary teaching about the kingdom of God in which He 'ups the grace ante' with His teaching on every part of life. Each word of this sermon was provocative and counter-cultural, but none more so that His command to '"Love your enemies'! –Mike Baker, Monday's reading.

- "Our Savior on the cross could have called down legions of angels and ended once and for all His suffering and the ridicule of the small people who mocked Him; instead, He filled that ugly six hours of pain with overwhelming grace. Elisha, like our Lord, responded with the steadfast kindness of God. He instructed Jehoram to prepare a table of feed for these enemies. Instead of a great slaughter, a great feast was offered, and, to everyone's amazement, Syria no longer bullied Israel (6:23). Love is like that." –J.K. Jones, Tuesday's reading.

- "We have found riches just beyond the borders. We have an inexhaustible supply of everything we need in Jesus Christ. And if we are subject to our selfish nature, we'll seek to hoard it while people go hungry. But we have been changed by the love of Christ. By God's grace, we'll even take the good news to those who have rejected us, in hopes that they will not reject Christ. The famine has turned into a feast. Get the word out!" –Jim Probst, Wednesday's reading.

- "Satan's tactics move in opposition to our theme of ridiculous love. He desires for us to hate, to marginalize, and to retaliate. The good news is that we can stand firm against his schemes. Our adversary is no match for our advocate and King, Jesus. We get to fight from a place of victory because of the ridiculous love Jesus demonstrated for us on the cross. While we were at our very worst, God gave us His best so that we could experience life to the fullest (Romans 5:8)." –Matt Fogel, Thursday's reading.

- "In this passage, Paul gives four negative imperatives (including positive counterparts) for addressing those who threaten us, oppose us, or cause us harm:
    1) "Bless those who persecute you; bless and **do not curse them**" (vs. 14).
    2) "**Repay no one evil for evil**, but give thought to do what is honorable in the sight of all" (vs. 17).
    3) "Beloved, **never avenge yourselves**, but leave it to the wrath of God [...] if your enemy is hungry, feed him; if he is thirsty, give him something to drink" (vs. 19-20).
    4) "**Do not be overcome by evil**, but overcome evil with good" (vs. 21). –Jim Probst, Friday's reading.

- "Today's Christian discipline is confession. The primary word in the New Testament for this practice in 'homologia.' It literally means to 'say the same thing.' It involves taking what is hidden in us and declaring it publicly." –J.K. Jones, Saturday's reading.

PART TWO: DISCUSS

PERSONALIZE YOUR DISCUSSION STARTER

Choose one of the following to engage your group in discussion:

- Name some of the greatest rivalries in sports (teams or individuals). Describe the greatest rivalry you've experienced.
- Name two of your "top 5" favorite movies of all time.

DIG IN DEEPER

1 Of the six chapters in this book, which do you find to be the most challenging? Why?

2 Take a moment to read the "summarize" section of this week's study.

3 Invite someone in the group to begin the study by leading the group in prayer.

4 Watch the video for week four, "Beyond the Borders: How do we love those who hate us?"

5 What challenged you most in this video teaching? What concepts should be remembered?

6 How does the story of Elisha demonstrate the heart of God in people? Re-read the excerpt from Tuesday's daily reading to get the discussion going.

7 Were you familiar with the story of the lepers prior to this Wednesday's reading? How did this story speak to you?

8 What hinders people most when faced with the opportunity to love their enemies? Is the same true for you?

9 What additional Scriptures and principles should be considered as we endeavor to love those who don't love us?

PART THREE: MOBILIZE

1 Take a moment to read Romans 12:14-21 and to review the excerpt from Friday's daily reading. How does the teaching from Romans 12:14-21 become an action point in your life?

2 Begin discussing ways in which you and your group can show the love of Christ to those who oppose you or are indifferent to you.

 • Brainstorm tangible expressions of love in the community.
 • Set a date for the group to model such love within the next two weeks.

3 Pray as a group, asking God to direct you as you demonstrate "ridiculous love" to those who do not love you.

FAMILY GUIDE

FAMILY FOCUS VERSE

Matthew 5:44
"But I say to you, love your enemies and pray for those who hurt you because of me."

FAMILY FAITH DISCUSSIONS

- The use of the term "enemies" can be a bit abstract for younger children, but upper elementary through high school will get the idea. Older children might actually have those who "oppose" them in the literal spirit of the text.
- Ask your kids about their "enemies." Let them talk to you about people in their lives, young or old, who are mean to them or have hurt them. Listen sympathetically.
- Do not dismiss their perceptions or their feelings. This will help them identify you as a safe person to talk to without judgment. However, gently help them realize that sometimes people are mean because of something in their life that is difficult for them to handle.
- Ask them how they can show kindness to those who are not kind to them.
- Close your discussion by having them pray for those who are hurting them.

Keep it short. Keep it simple. Keep it real.

STUDENT MINISTRY PARENT GUIDE

BIG IDEA

From Monday's reading: "Each word of the [Sermon on the Mount] sermon was provocative and counter-cultural but none more so than his command to 'Love your enemies'!" Through your humble guidance and modeling—your student(s) too can love their enemies and show the love of Jesus to the world.

DAILY REFLECTIONS

• **Monday:** "Believing that Jesus is the ultimate truth makes some hate us because they want to be justified in doing things their own way. They want to believe their own truth and believe it's just as good for them as any way of life." Why do you believe the Jesus-following-life is unique and most satisfying? Who are you praying for and choosing to love that hates you? This week, ask your student who they are choosing to love that previously had judged them for the way they acted or looked or done against them previously. Be real and share how you are choosing to love your enemies in your life. Don't underestimate the power of a little transparency with your teenager.

• **Thursday:** "We get to fight from a place of victory because of the ridiculous love Jesus demonstrated on the cross." What would the difference be in your family if you led out from victory instead of for victory? Why does your teenager need this timeless truth in their arsenal of love as they choose to love their enemies?

WEEKLY DISCIPLINE

• **Saturday:** Confession–Your teenager probably needs to confess to you for their attitude, disrespect, apathy at home, and unwillingness to learn from discipline. But what would it look like for you to take the first step in confession? When was the last time you apologized when you were wrong towards your teenager? Often, students just want to be heard and validated on their thoughts. Your humility in saying a simple "sorry" and intentional prayer for your hormonal teenager could repair much of what's been strained.

CAMPUS MINISTRY GUIDE

DAILY REFLECTIONS

In many ways, college is the time where we define our borders. Borders signify who is in and who is out. Often it is simplest to define borders by who stands 'with' us and who stands 'against' us. Before going into the questions this week, spend some time thinking and identifying the borders you have constructed and who falls outside those borders.

- **Tuesday:** What are the greatest "victories of love" that I can recall? Are they stories of nations, stories of organizations, stories of family members and friends, maybe even personal stories? Where have I seen love conquer vengeance?
- **Friday:** What happens when we choose to love those who have wronged us (parents, professors, former friends or significant others)?
- **Saturday:** Confession = "to agree with what God has already said about us" – is there a type of confession that is new to me this week? Try and focus just on this new aspect of confession for the next week.

WEEK FIVE
BELOW THE STREETS
(Why does the Bible tell me not to love the world?)

PART ONE: SUMMARIZE

1 John 2:15 says, "Do not love the world or the things of the world." Yet, we are in a world saturated with slick advertisements, self-serving slogans, and a worldview that compels us to crave more and more of it. In this week's reading, we are reminded that "ridiculous" love is characterized by an increased appetite and affection for the things of Heaven and a growing dissatisfaction with the things of the world.

KEY QUOTES FROM THE VIDEO TEACHING

- "He is away from familiarity, he is away from his home, and yet Daniel still stands up for what he believes is right." –Mike Baker

- "Amidst all the chaos of being in Babylon and the sewer-like life that was going on there, we've got a guy who is resolved to do what God wants him to do." –J.K. Jones

- "If you and I are going to be the people that God wants us to be, we're going to have to stop valuing what the world values. We're going to have to change our value system." –Mike Baker

- "When Daniel resolves, it is not just a negative thing. He's also bringing in the sovereignty of God in his resolution." –J.K. Jones

- "We're actually calling you to inaction. What would it be like to fast from something as a response to this great teaching today? I want you guys to consider in your small groups [...] whether or not you could have an intentional fast as individuals and maybe collectively as a group. How can you hold each other accountable to that? How can you fast so that you can feast on the Lord?" –Jim Probst

KEY QUOTES FROM THE DAILY READING

- "But this rejecting of worldly things is ridiculous only if you have not embraced the ridiculous love of Jesus. For those who have, there is nothing in this world that can compete with the love of God in Christ Jesus." –Mike Baker, Monday's reading.

- "In spite of the fall of Jerusalem, in spite of the victory of Babylon over Israel, in spite of the exile from the Promised Land into a pagan culture, and in spite of all the evidence that seemed to support the conclusion that the gods of Babylon were superior to the God of Israel, there remained an unshakeable confidence on the part of these four young men in the sovereign God of the universe." –J.K. Jones, Tuesday's reading.

- "This world is tantalizing and alluring. Our hearts get ensnared in the trappings of temporal pursuits and distracted and dissuaded from the life of a follower. 'Prosperity knits a man to the World,' and the clamoring and calling of every commercial compels us to forsake followership. We lay down our nets only to pick them up in a season of uncertainty, just like Peter." –Jim Probst, Wednesday's reading.

- "Think Romans 6:1. 'Are we to continue in sin that grace may abound'? Like Paul, Jude gives this hearty response, 'By no means'! Grace is the means to forgiveness and ushers in the necessary power to wage war against sin. It is not a license to live in a 'whatever' way in a 'whatever' world. Grace encourages obedience." –J.K. Jones, Thursday's reading.

- "Verse 21 reads, "Little children, keep yourselves from idols" (1 John 5:21). This is a timeless truth communicated to the church of the first century and the twenty first century. Idolatry can shipwreck the light, life, and love that infiltrate this entire letter. John was concerned about the false gods that had flooded the culture and seeped into the church." –Jim Probst, Friday's reading.

• "We might choose to fast because we recognize a need for spiritual renewal. Think of Nehemiah 9:1-2 and how Israel had returned from Babylonian captivity and needed to affirm her renewed commitment to covenant-living. Sometimes we fast because we desire guidance and direction from God. Consider Esther 4:16. An evil plot had been hatched by the villain Haman to kill all the Jews. Prompted by her Uncle Mordecai, Queen Esther called for a three day fast. Perhaps we fast because a situation in the life of the church prompts a unique season of seeking God. Think Acts 13:1-3." –J.K. Jones, Saturday's reading.

PART TWO: DISCUSS

PERSONALIZE YOUR DISCUSSION STARTER

Choose one of the following to engage your group in discussion:

• Would it be harder for you to go without food or without sleep for the next 36 hours?
• What enjoyable hobby do you currently sacrifice for more pressing or important priorities in this season of life?

DIG IN DEEPER

1 Invite someone in the group to begin this study with prayer for the group. Consider paraphrasing John 17:14-19 in this time of prayer.

2 As a group, read the "summarize" section of this week's study.

3 Watch the video for week five, "Below the Streets: Why does the Bible tell me not to love the world?"

4 How do you think you would have responded if you were Daniel or his friends?

5 What are modern-day situations you face that parallel Daniel's situation? Explain.

6 Do you agree with the key quote from Monday's reading? Why?

7 In reference to Wednesday's reading, how do you see "prosperity knitting a man's heart to the world," as C.S. Lewis observed? Has there ever been a culture more inclined to the trap of prosperity than ours?

8 How does 1 John 5:21 speak to this issue of not loving the world?

9 Is there something about this world that is becoming less appealing to you as you grow in your love for God and His Kingdom?

PART THREE: MOBILIZE

1 Review the teaching from Saturday's daily reading. What questions do you have about fasting?

2 How does "fasting from the things of the world" and "feasting on the things of God" work together?

3 Commit to fast from something this week. Share your example with the group before the end of this day. Be specific.

4 Are there any additional Scriptures or practices in the group that might be helpful regarding this topic?

5 Conclude this group discussion by praying in pairs, looking to encourage one another in this decision to "love not the world" this week.

FAMILY GUIDE

FAMILY FOCUS VERSE

1 John 2:15
"Do not love the world or the things of the world."

FAMILY FAITH DISCUSSIONS

- If you have older kids, you can jump right in with asking them how we can obey God to love the world, but not love the things of this world.
- If you have younger kids, you will want to discuss how the "things of this world" are the things that pull us away from God and want us to live in ways God doesn't want us to live.
- Take this as an opportunity to discuss their circle of friends, their choice in music or the shows they like to watch, the clothes they wear, etc. Without preaching to them right away, let them tell you what they see in those things that are "of the world," letting them arrive at some conclusions themselves... then fill in the gaps as needed.
- Tell a shortened version of the story of Daniel.
- Pick something as a family, perhaps the same thing your small group chose, to fast from this week. Use it as an opportunity for some extra family time and make some memories.

Keep it short. Keep it simple. Keep it real.

STUDENT MINISTRY PARENT GUIDE

BIG IDEA

There are a slew of voices competing for your son or daughter's affections and attention, promising a fuller life if only they would [...] Some are more subtle than others, but all make the same empty claims. Christ offers a different way: The way of the Gospel. And it is only through this good news of Jesus that your student(s) can be satisfied—not by loving the world, but by embracing the ridiculous love of Jesus.

DAILY REFLECTIONS

- **Tuesday:** "The One who created us and called us into the kingdom of light has named us His children. We are kids of the King, and our identity is found in Him. Do not love the world." What do you see your student(s) loving in this world, that is leaving them empty and unsatisfied? How could you come alongside them and help them replace the destructive with the divine?

- **Wednesday:** The quote from C.S. Lewis' Screwtape Letters speaks of the way we make this world our comfortable self-centered home. In what ways does your family live too comfortably in this world? How might possessions or a certain quality of life play into your student's struggles with loving the world more than God? Is God someone your family prioritizes only on Sundays or does he permeate everything you do Sunday through Saturday?

WEEKLY DISCIPLINE

- **Saturday:** Fasting–It is highly likely that your teenager has a phone. Although cell phones can be a life saving resource, they can also be a huge idol for teenagers—distracting and deceiving them in a host of different ways. Try challenging the entire family to do a "phone fast." Cast vision to your family WHY you feel led by God to do this, and challenge everyone to turn off their phones after a certain time at night and leave them in a basket so they won't be tempted to check them. Maybe do it on family night or all day Sunday—maybe just during dinnertime. Help your teenager learn how to properly steward and control their things, so that their things don't control them.

CAMPUS MINISTRY GUIDE

DAILY REFLECTIONS

The Campus Community and College Years are filled with "subtle messages" about our identity. With so much identity formation happening in college, what are the costs of silencing the "Jesus-voice" through the college years? So many students take a "break" from faith in college only to find that they form an identity completely void of Jesus. What campus messages are competing with Jesus for your identity?

- **Wednesday:** How can college put a laundry list of "temporal prizes" ahead of our primary purpose? Have I ever noticed how "easily entangled" my heart, mind and soul can get with the things of campus and the world?
- **Friday:** "An idol is any substitute for God" – have I ever labeled the things that I substitute for God as idols (food, money, sex, power, success, recognition, pleasure, etc)? What does thinking about these things as "false gods" do to my affinity for them?
- **Saturday:** Fasting = "an exercise of self-denial and dependence on God" – when it comes to setting aside my idols, do I struggle more in the self-denial or the dependence aspect? How could regular rhythms of fasting increase my appetite for God without becoming a legalistic ritual?

WEEK SIX
BENEATH THE CROSS
(What's the big deal about the cross?)

PART ONE: SUMMARIZE

Perhaps the most "ridiculous" moment in history was when the Righteous One faced ridicule on a cross. This love is initiated by the Father, incarnate in the Son, and to be imitated by those who follow after Him. If our King risked the "ridiculous," why would we risk anything less?

KEY QUOTES FROM THE VIDEO TEACHING

- "One of the remarkable things that we've been trying to unpack is this characteristic of God, God's love. But that love is matched by this – He's a warrior. He's willing to do whatever needs to be done in order to accomplish His great love." –J.K. Jones

- "The Israelites were not immune to the death angel. God's justice demands that He's going to punish sinfulness. And the Egyptians were sinful; they were not God's people. But even God's people were sinful. And so something had to take place to keep them from being punished for their sin." –Mike Baker

- "What God was doing was giving them a 2-3 million person object lesson. He was painting a picture for what He was going to do in the future because of his Son, Jesus Christ." –Mike Baker

- "God is love. He's also just. And so only the genius of God could say, 'I can accomplish both things at once. I can sacrifice a lamb that's perfect, and I can show my love for those who are lost. I can also pay for and have justice served for all the sins. So there's just not a greater picture of the slaughtered lamb in the Old Testament that leads to the Lamb on the cross in the New Testament that leads to the resurrected Lamb in the Book of Revelation." –Mike Baker

• "As we wrap things up, we are just reminded again that we live in a love-starved world. But we also know the ridiculous love of Jesus, and we've experienced it. The challenge as we move forward with the end of this study is that we can communicate that ridiculous love of Christ to the world around. It is the Great Commission." –Jim Probst

KEY QUOTES FROM THE DAILY READING

• "The cross is the place where I am motivated to love ridiculously. Now that I understand how much I have been loved, what can I do but love others in the same way? Jesus begins and ends this teaching on laying down His live with a command for how His followers should respond to His great sacrifice: 'This is my commandment, that you love one another as I have loved you' (John 15:12). 'These things I command you, so that you will love one another' (John 15-17). I believe this was intentional because this is the why and how for my love towards others." –Mike Baker, Monday's reading.

• "The love of Jesus Christ, like the original Passover lamb, was literally spilled out in and through the blood running down the cross, covered by the sin and shame of all of us, bathed in darkness. I can hardly see the screen on my PC because the thought of that image grabs my heart and brings tears to my eyes. More darkness, more blood, sin abounding. Ridiculous love." –J.K. Jones, Tuesday's reading.

• In reference to 1 John 5:11-13, "Why does John write 'these things'? He does so that we 'may know that we have eternal life.' It is by His work on the cross that this author, giver, and sustainer of life authenticated His message, bringing victory over the grave. It is 'in Him' that we are rooted, 'by Him' that we love, and 'for Him' that we live. 'These things' are listed throughout this letter, giving indicators that we are His and becoming more like Him." –Jim Probst, Wednesday's reading.

• "Hallelujah! I mean that with all the gusto I can muster. Praise Him for what He did! Christ on the cross completely disarmed and destroyed all the spiritual powers that would lay claim over us. Christ's triumph is our triumph." –J.K. Jones, Thursday's reading.

• "Like the Jew and Gentiles of long ago, many of us bring our own bias and expectation to the table. We are looking for the king of our making, rather than the King of Kings. The cross is still at the cross-roads of faith for each and every one of us. Was Jesus a victim or the victor on that dark day? Was He without sign and wisdom, or was the cross the great sign and wisdom of the gather, anticipated from the beginning of time and orchestrated flawlessly through the Savior?" –Jim Probst, Friday's reading.

• "Witnessing, at its very core, is simply sharing the love of Christ with those around us that we ourselves have already experienced from Him. We witness to His love on the cross. We witness to the change His love has made in us. We witness to His love by indiscriminately sharing His story and His love with those we meet. Our fundamental desire is to love the way Jesus loved and loves, right?" –J.K. Jones, Saturday's reading.

PART TWO: DISCUSS

PERSONALIZE YOUR DISCUSSION STARTER

Choose one of the following to engage your group in discussion:

• Think of the most recognizable symbols or logos in the world. Nike, Coca-Cola, and McDonalds come to mind. How well known is the cross in comparison? Is there another image that is more widely known?

• Think about how different your life might be in ten years. What things will remain the same? What will be the most significant change? Write your answers on a note card and place them in a cup. Randomly read each one, guessing who wrote each one.

DIG IN DEEPER

1 As a group, read Exodus 12:21-32.

2 Watch the video for week six, "Beneath the Cross: What's the big deal about the cross?"

3 Do you find it difficult to discuss the story about the Passover? How would it be received by a friend who doesn't know Christ?

4 Read the third key quote from the video teaching. Does the "object lesson" still apply today? Are there any barriers to grasping the message of the Passover? Explain.

5 What Scripture references or writings did you find most helpful this week? Why?

6 Read 1 John 5:11-13. How does this passage intersect with the commonly-held opinion that "all roads lead to heaven"?

7 Read 1 Corinthians 1:18-25 as a group. How does this passage speak to our society today?

PART THREE: MOBILIZE

1 Why do you think "witnessing" is so rarely practiced by Christians?

2 Review the teaching from Saturday's daily reading. Which of the "six practical suggestions" are most challenging to you? Why?

3 What is a challenging and reasonable expectation for you and your group to establish regarding witnessing? Discuss and prayerfully commit to a course of action.

4 What is the "next step" for you and your small group at the conclusion of this study? What will you study next? How will you proceed?

5 Conclude this group discussion by praying as a group. Consider joining hands in a circle, facing outward as a visible demonstration of the unity and witness your group desires. Humbly ask God to use you to share hope with those apart from Christ.

FAMILY GUIDE

FAMILY FOCUS VERSE

John 15: 13
"Greater love has no one than this, that he lay down his life for his friends."

FAMILY FAITH DISCUSSIONS

- This week has the opportunity for you to teach the gospel to your kids. Even if they've heard it many times before, we all need to be reminded of God's grace and gift to us in Jesus.
- Discuss with your kids how they can ask God to forgive them, and He will do that.
- With older children, ask, "then why did Jesus have to go through all that if God will just forgive us?" Use Mike's teaching on justice and love (Key quotes) to help explain that when someone sins in this world, someone has to pay for it. God just didn't want it to be us.
- Read John 15:13 and talk about how your family can "lay down our lives for Jesus." What sacrifices can we make to be all about doing God's work in this world?
- After this study, it would be a great time for your family (young and old) to write a simple *family mission statement* that guides your values, decisions, and activities as a family. Put it on your fridge, paint it on the wall, or frame it and hang it the bathroom: somewhere where everyone is reminded often of what your family is all about.

Keep it short. Keep it simple. Keep it real.

STUDENT MINISTRY PARENT GUIDE

BIG IDEA

Monday's reading clearly ties everything together with the quote, "the cross is the place where I was loved ridiculously." Pray this week for ways to talk about and exemplify sacrificial love to your kids, that they would embrace the same kind of life—one laid down, because Jesus laid His down first.

DAILY REFLECTIONS

- **Tuesday:** "The shed blood of Jesus made it eternally possible for anyone and everyone to place their trust in the finished work of Christ." How often do you talk about the cross in your home, in your prayers, in your counseling sessions with your teens? Do you think they comprehend what the cross means for their life?

- **Wednesday:** "The road is narrow, long and winding. The way is difficult and demanding. Our journey home is impossible apart from Him." The looming statistic is that somewhere around 50% of Christian students walk away from their faith while in college. One of the reasons why many researchers have found this to be true is the truth found in the quote above. Whether you have a 7th grader or a junior in high school, how can you be preparing them for the tough road ahead of faith? What types of relationships could you point them to? What kinds of conversations do you need to have? What kind of open-book environment could you create in your house for questions and wrestling? What kind of spiritual climate do you want to kindle now so that they would have deep roots for this difficult journey of faith?

WEEKLY DISCIPLINE

- **Saturday:** Witnessing–How could you reach out to your neighbors as a family this week? Have your kids creatively brainstorm together with you. Pray together as a family, and even make the invite to church together one evening.

CAMPUS MINISTRY GUIDE

DAILY REFLECTIONS

By the time we get to college, we have encountered the story of Jesus' cross too often to really be amazed by it. Stop and think about the two aspects of this love that are highlighted in Monday's reading: 1) It is love that drove a man to death; 2) It is a one-sided love. How does this love inspire me to love more ridiculously?

- **Wednesday:** How is a relationship with Jesus getting me through the tough roads of college? How does His supreme promise of eternal life motivate me to meet my everyday challenges (classes, relationships, future plans)?
- **Friday:** "Victim or victor" – how do I interpret the cross?
- **Saturday:** Witnessing = "sharing the love of Christ with those around us that we ourselves have already experienced" – is it possible to be a good witness without a constant attachment to the ridiculous love of Jesus? Within our attempts to share the love of Christ on our Campuses, let us make sure that we are experiencing the love which we are seeking to share.

WORKS CITED

Bright, Bill. (1995). *Basic Steps to Successful Fasting & Prayer.* Orlando: New Life Publications.

Hooper, Walter. (Ed.) (1996). *C.S. Lewis: Reading for Meditation and Reflection.* San Francisco: HarperCollins Publishers.

Ingram, Chip. (2006). *God As He Longs for You to See Him.* Grand Rapids: Baker Books.

Manning, Brennan. (2009). *The Furious Longing of God.* Colorado Springs: David C. Cook.

Moody, Dwight L. Moody, Dwight L. (2014). Retrieved April 2, 2014, from *BrainyQuote.com.* Xplore, Inc.

Peterson, Eugene. (2011). *The Pastor.* New York: HarperOne.

Piper, John. (2006). *Fifty Reasons Why Jesus Came to Die.* Wheaton: Crossway Books.

Ryken, Phil. (2012). *Loving the Way Jesus Loves.* Wheaton: Crossway Books.

Trotman, Dawson. (1955). *Born to Reproduce.* Colorado Springs: The Navigators.

Zempel, Heather. (2012). *Community is Messy.* Downers Grove: IVP Books.

ABOUT THE AUTHORS

This book represents just a portion of the entire "Ridiculous" all-church study, originally designed for Eastview Christian Church. The authors for this project have invested countless hours in prayer, preparation and presentation of this material. I count it a remarkable privilege and honor to live out these concepts with such a dedicated team of servant leaders. For more information about the authors and ministries, visit our website at www.eastviewchurch.net.

Mike Baker	Senior Pastor
J.K. Jones, Jr.	Pastor of Spiritual Formation
Jim Probst	Pastor of Small Groups

SPECIAL THANKS

Thank you to all of the hard-working and creative individuals who have helped to create not only the "Ridiculous" book, but the videos and small group discussions for this series! As always, a project of this magnitude requires more team members and "behind the scenes help" than can be listed. However, I want to specifically thank Karen Norris and Alyssa Deffner for their tireless creative energy in developing the artwork and concepts for the book and videos that truly amaze me. Thanks also to Scott Sarver and Shawn Prokes for their video expertise! Thank you to Caleb Baker, Matt Fogle and Charlie Welke for their contributions with the study guide and daily devotions. Thank you also to Julie Pond for her copy editing work on this project. I'm thankful for the elders and members of Eastview Christian Church who've already demonstrated ridiculous love to thousands in this community! And finally, thank you to Mike Baker and J.K. Jones for their teaching and leadership. It's truly an honor to serve with such ridiculous people.

In Christ,
Jim Probst